Missouri's
Bicycle Trails

Includes Metro Kansas City & Metro St. Louis

D1069405

An American Bike Trails Publication

Missouri's
Bicycle Trails

Includes Metro Kansas City & Metro St. Louis

Published by   American Bike Trails

Copyright 2007 by   American Bike Trails

Created by   Ray Hoven

Illustrated & Designed by   Mary C. Rumpsa

Table of Contents

St. Louis Metropolitan Area

Kansas City Metropolitian Area – Missouri

Table of Contents (continued)

Kansas City Metropolitian Area – Missouri (continued)

Kansas City Metropolitan Area – Kansas

Northern Missouri

Southern Missouri

Indexes

How to Use this Book

This book provides a comprehensive, easy-to use reference to the many off-road trails throughout Missouri. It contains over 70 detailed trails maps. The book is organized by geographical sections: St. Louis Metro, Kansas City Metro, Northern and Southern Missouri. St. Louis Metro includes Madison County, Illinois. Kansas City Metro includes Leavenworth, Wyandotte, Johnson, Douglas, Miami, Franklin and Osage counties. Each section begins with a map of that section showing trail locations together with a reference listing of trails within the section. The back of the book provides indexes in alphabetical sequence of all the trails illustrated, plus separate listings by leisure and mountain biking, and cross references by city to trail and county to trail. The trail maps include such helpful features as locations and access, trail facilities, and nearby communities.

Bicycle Safety

Bicycling offers many rewards, among them a physically fit body and a pleasant means of transportation. But the sport has its hazards, which can lead to serious accidents and injuries. We have provided rules, facts and tips that can help minimize the dangers of bicycling while you're having fun.

Choose The Right Bicycle
Adults and children should ride bicycles with frames small enough to be straddled easily with both feet flat on the ground, and with handlebars that can be easily reached with elbows bent. Oversize bikes make it difficult to ride comfortably and maintain control. Likewise, don't buy a large bike for a child to grow into--smaller is safer.

Learn To Ride The Safe Way
When learning to ride a bike, let a little air out of the tires, and practice steering and balancing by "scootering" around with both feet on the ground and the seat as low as possible. The "fly-or-fall" method-where someone runs alongside the bicycle and then lets go-can result in injuries.

Training wheels don't work, since the rider can't learn to balance until the wheels come of. They can be used with a timid rider, but the child still will have to learn to ride without them. Once the rider can balance and pedal (without training wheels), raise the seat so that the rider's leg is almost straight at the bottom of the pedal stroke.

Children seldom appreciate the dangers and hazards of city cycling. Make sure they understand the traffic laws before letting them onto the road.

Use This Important Equipment
Headlight A working headlight and rear reflector are required for night riding in some states. Side reflectors do not make the rider visible to drivers on cross streets.

Safety seat for children under 40 lbs. Make sure the seat is mounted firmly over the rear wheel of the bike, and does not wobble when going downhill at high speed. Make sure the child will not slide down while riding. The carrier should also have a device to keep the child's feet from getting into the spokes.

Package rack Racks are inexpensive, and they let the rider steer with both hands and keep packages out of the spokes.

Beware Of Dangerous Practices
Never ride against traffic. Failure to observe this rule causes the majority of car-bicycle collisions. Motorists can't always avoid the maneuvers of a wrong-way rider since the car and bike move toward each other very quickly.

Never make a left turn from the right lane.

Never pass through an intersection at full speed.

Never ignore stop light or stop signs.

Never enter traffic suddenly from a driveway or sidewalk. This rule is particularly important when the rider is a child, who is more difficult for a motorist to see.

Don't wear headphones that make it hard to hear and quickly respond to traffic.

Don't carry passengers on a bike. The only exception is a child under 40 lbs. who is buckled into an approved bike safety seat and wears a helmet as required by law.

Passenger trailers can be safe and fun. Be aware, though, that a trailer makes the bike much longer and requires careful control. Passengers must wear helmets.

Get A Bike That Works With You
Skilled riders who use their bikes often for exercise or transport should consider buying multi-geared bikes, which increase efficiency while minimizing stress on the body. (These bikes may not be appropriate for young or unskilled riders, who may concentrate more on the gears than on the road.) The goal is to keep the pedals turning at a rate of 60-90 RPM. Using the higher gears while pedaling slowly is hard on the knees, and is slower and more tiring than the efficient pedaling on the experienced cyclist. Have a safe trip!

What To Look For In A Bicycle Helmet
We endorse these guidelines for bicycle helmets recommended by the American Academy of Pediatrics:

The helmet should meet the voluntary testing standards of one of these two groups: American National Standards Institute (ANSI) OR Snell Memorial Foundation. Look for a sticker on the inside of the helmet.

1.) Select the right size. Find one that fits comfortably and doesn't pinch.

2.) Buy a helmet with a durable outer shell and a polystyrene liner. Be sure it allows adequate ventilation.

3.) Use the adjustable foam pads to ensure a proper fit at the front, back and sides.

4.) Adjust the strap for a snug fit. The helmet should cover the top of your

Bicycle Safety (continued)

forehead and not rock side to side or back and forth with the chain strap in place.

5.) Replace your helmet if it is involved in an accident.

Emergency Toolkit

When venturing out on bicycle tours, it is always smart to take along equipment to help make roadside adjustments and repairs. It is not necessary for every member of your group to carry a complete set of equipment, but make sure someone in your group brings along the equipment listed below:

1.) Standard or slotted screwdriver
2.) Phillips screwdriver
3.) 6" or 8" adjustable wrench
4.) Small pliers
5.) Spoke adjuster
6.) Tire pressure gauge
7.) Portable tire pump
8.) Spare innertube
9.) Tire-changing lugs

A Few Other Things

When embarking on a extended bike ride, it is important to give your bike a pre-ride check. To ensure that your bike is in premium condition, go over the bike's mechanisms, checking for any mechanical problems. It's best to catch these at home, and not when they occur "on the road." If you run into a problem that you can't fix yourself, you should check your local yellow pages for a professional bike mechanic.

When you are planning a longer trip, be sure to consider your own abilities and limitations, as well as those of any companions who may be riding with you. In general, you can ride about three times the length (time-wise) as your average training ride. If you have a regular cycling routine, this is a good basis by which to figure the maximum distance you can handle.

Finally, be aware of the weather. Bring plenty of sunblock for clear days, and rain gear for the rainy one. Rain can make some rides miserable, in addition to making it difficult to hear other traffic. Winds can blow up sand, and greatly increase the difficulty of a trail.

Trail Courtesy & Common Sense

1.) Stay on designated trails.

2.) Bicyclists use the right side of the trail (Walkers use the left side of the trail).

3.) Bicyclists should only pass slower users on the left side of the trail; use your voice to warn others when you need to pass.

4.) Get off to the side of the trail if you need to stop.

5.) Bicyclists should yield to all other users.

6.) Do not use alcohol or drugs while on the trail.

7.) Do not litter.

8.) Do not trespass onto adjacent land.

9.) Do not wear headphones while using the trail.

Health Hazards

Hypothermia

Hypothermia is a condition where the core body temperature falls below 90 degrees. This may cause death.

Mild hypothermia

Symptoms	a. Pronounced shivering
	b. Loss of physical coordination
	c. Thinking becomes cloudy

Causes   a. Cold, wet, loss of body heat, wind

Treatment
- a. Prevent further heat loss, get out of wet clothing and out of wind. Replace wet clothing with dry.
- b. Help body generate more heat. Refuel with high-energy foods and a hot drink, get moving around, light exercise, or external heat.

Severe hypothermia

Symptoms
- a. Shivering stops, pulse and respiration slows down, speech becomes incoherent.

Treatment
- a. Get help immediately.
- b. Don't give food or water.
- c. Don't try to rewarm the victim in the field.
- d. A buildup of toxic wastes and tactic acid accumulates in the blood in the body's extremities. Movement or rough handling will cause a flow of the blood from the extremities to the heart. This polluted blood can send the heart into ventricular fibrillations (heart attack), and may result in death.
- e. Wrap victim in several sleeping bags and insulate from the ground.

Frostbite

Symptoms of frostbite may include red skin with white blotches due to lack of circulation. Rewarm body parts gently. Do not immerse in hot water or rub to restore circulation, as both will destroy skin cell.

Health Hazards (continued)

Heat Exhaustion

Cool, pale, and moist skin, heavy sweating, headache, nausea, dizziness and vomiting. Body temperature nearly normal.

Treatment   Have victim lie in the coolest place available– on back with feet raised. Rub body gently with cool, wet cloth. Give person   glass of water every 15 minutes if conscious and can tolerate it. Call for emergency medical assistance.

Heat Stroke

Hot, red skin, shock or unconsciousness; high body temperature.

Treatment   Treat as a life-threatening emergency. Call for emergency medical assistance immediately. Cool victim by any means possible. Cool bath, pour cool water over body, or wrap wet sheets around body. Give nothing by mouth.

West Nile Virus

West Nile Virus is transmitted by certain types of mosquitoes. Most people infected with West Nile Virus won't develop symptoms. Some may become ill 3 to 15 days after being bitten.

Protect Yourself   Wear proper clothing, use insect repellents and time your outdoor activities to reduce your risk of mosquito bites and other insect problems. Most backyard mosquito problems are caused by mosquitoes breeding in and around homes, not those from more natural areas.

Trail Related Terms

Length Expressed in miles one way. Round trip mileage is normally indicated for loops.

Effort Levels *Easy* Physical exertion is not strenuous. Climbs and descents as well as technical obstacles are more minimal. Recommended for beginners.

Moderate Physical exertion is not excessive. Climbs and descents can be challenging. Expect some technical obstacles.

Difficult Physical exertion is demanding. Climbs and descents require good riding skills. Trail surface may be sandy, loose rock, soft or wet.

Directions Describes by way of directions and distances, how to get to the trail areas from roads and nearby communities.

Map Illustrative representation of a geographic area, such as a state, section, forest, park or trail complex.

DNR Department of Natural Resources

DOT Department of Transportation

11

Definition of Geological & Geographic Terms

Bog　　　　An acidic wetland that is fed by rainwater and is characterized by open water with a floating mat of vegetation (e.g. sedges, mosses, tamarack) that will often bounce if you jump on it.

Bluff　　　 A high steep bank with a broad, flat, or rounded front.

Canyon　　A deep, narrow valley with precipitous sides, often with a stream flowing through it.

Drumlin　　Smooth oval hill of glacial drift, elongated in the direction of the movement of the ice that deposited it. Drumlins may be more than 150 feet high and more than a half mile long.

Esker　　　A long winding, serpentine ridge of glacial drift (gravel) with steep sides (10-50 feet high).

Fen　　　　An alkaline wetland that is fed by ground water and is often seen as a wet meadow and characterized by plants like Grass or Parnasis and sedges that grow in alkaline water.

Forest　　 A vegetative community dominated by trees and many containing understory layers of smaller trees, shorter shrubs and an herbaceous layers at the ground.

Grove　　 A small wooded area without underbrush, such as a picnic area.

Herb　　　A seed producing annual, biennial, or perennial that does not develop persistent woody tissue but dies down at the end of a growing season.

Kame　　 An oval depression of glacial till, often filled with water, formed when buried and stranded chunks of ice from a retreating glacier melted.

Kettle　　 Oval depression found in glacial moraines, which are landforms made up of rock debris, which melts as the ground above it subsides, forming a kettle.

Lake　　　A considerable inland body of standing water.

Marsh　　 A wetland fed by streams and with shallow or deep water. Often characterized by mats of cattail, bulrushes, sedges and wetland forbs.

Mesic　　 A type of plant that requires a moderate amount of water.

Moraine	Long, irregular hills of glacial till deposited by stagnant and retreating glaciers.
Natural Community	A group of living organisms that live in the same place, e.g. woodland or prairie.
Park	An area maintained in its natural state as a public property.
Pond	A body of water usually smaller than a lake.
Prairie	Primarily treeless grassland community characterized by full sun and dominated by perennial, native grasses and forbs.
Preserve	An area restricted for the protection and preservation of natural resources.
Ridge	A range of hills or mountains.
Savanna	A grassland ecosystem with scattered trees characterized by native grasses and forbs.
Sedges	Grass-like plants with triangular stems and without showy flowers. Many are dominant in sedge meadows, bogs and fens but others are found in woodlands or prairies.
Shrubs	Low woody plants, usually shorter than trees and with several stems.
Swale	A lower lying or depressed and often wet stretch of land.
Swamp	Spongy land saturated and sometimes partially or intermittently covered with water.
Turf	The upper stratum of soil bound by grass and plant roots into a thick mat.
Wetland	The low lying wet area between higher ridges.

Explanation of Symbols

SYMBOL LEGEND

- 🏊 Beach/Swimming
- 🚲 Bicycle Repair
- 🏚 Cabin
- ⚠ Camping
- 🛶 Canoe Launch
- ✚ First Aid
- ⊕ Food
- GC Golf Course
- ? Information
- ⌂ Lodging
- MF Multi-Facilities
- P Parking
- 🏞 Picnic
- 🚶 Ranger Station
- 🚻 Restrooms
- ⌂ Shelter
- T Trailhead
- 🏛 Visitor Center
- 🚰 Water
- 🔭 Overlook/Observation

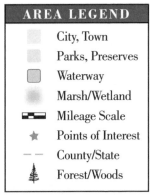

AREA LEGEND

- City, Town
- Parks, Preserves
- Waterway
- Marsh/Wetland
- ▬▬ Mileage Scale
- ★ Points of Interest
- ─ ─ County/State
- 🌲 Forest/Woods

TRAIL LEGEND

- ▬▬▬ Trail-Biking/Multi
- ············· Hiking only Trail
- ●●●●●●●●● Hiking - Multi Use
- ▬▬▬▬ Snowmobiling only
- = = = = = = Planned Trail
- ▬ ▬ ▬ ▬ Alternate Trail
- ▬▬▬ Road/Highway
- ++++++++++ Railroad Tracks

Missouri Sections

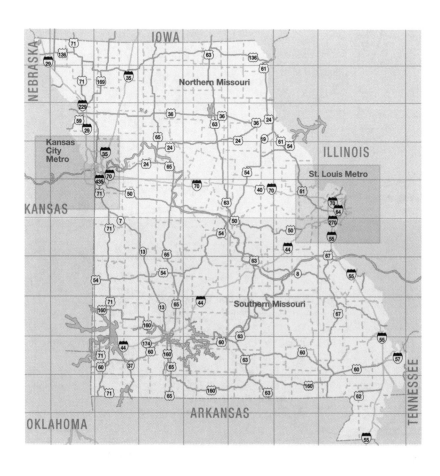

St. Louis Metropolitan Area

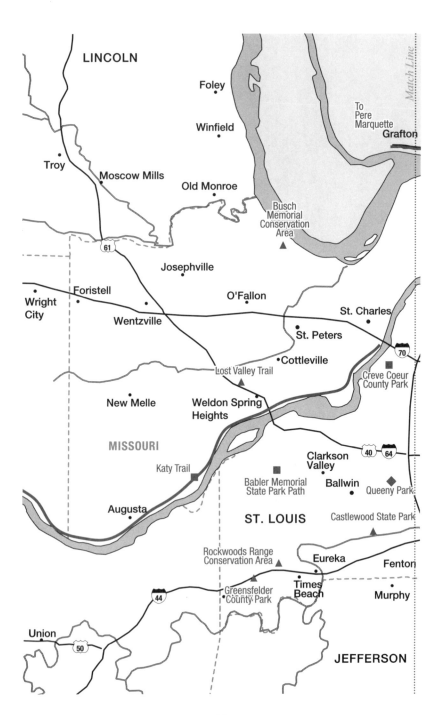

LINCOLN

Foley

Winfield

To Pere Marquette
Grafton

Troy

Moscow Mills

Old Monroe

Busch Memorial Conservation Area

61

Josephville

Foristell

O'Fallon

St. Charles

Wright City

Wentzville

St. Peters

70

Cottleville

Lost Valley Trail

Creve Coeur County Park

New Melle

Weldon Spring Heights

MISSOURI

Clarkson Valley

40 64

Katy Trail

Babler Memorial State Park Path

Ballwin

Queeny Park

Augusta

ST. LOUIS

Castlewood State Park

Rockwoods Range Conservation Area

Eureka

Fenton

Greensfelder County Park

44

Times Beach

Murphy

Union

50

JEFFERSON

Match Line

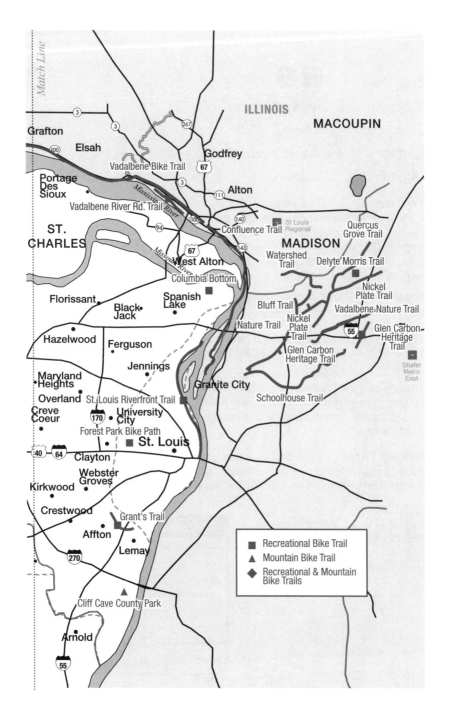

ILLINOIS

MACOUPIN

Grafton
Elsah
Godfrey
Vadalbene Bike Trail
Portage Des Sioux
Alton
Vadalbene River Rd. Trail
ST. CHARLES
Confluence Trail
St Louis Regional
Quercus Grove Trail
MADISON
Watershed Trail
Delyte Morris Trail
West Alton
Columbia Bottom
Nickel Plate Trail
Florissant
Spanish Lake
Bluff Trail
Vadalbene Nature Trail
Black Jack
Nature Trail
Nickel Plate Trail
Hazelwood
Ferguson
Glen Carbon Heritage Trail
Glen Carbon Heritage Trail
Jennings
Shafer Metro East
Maryland Heights
Granite City
Overland
St. Louis Riverfront Trail
Schoolhouse Trail
Creve Coeur
University City
Forest Park Bike Path
St. Louis
Clayton
Webster Groves
Kirkwood
Crestwood
Grant's Trail
Affton
Lemay
Cliff Cave County Park
Arnold

Mississippi River
Missouri River

Match Line

■ Recreational Bike Trail
▲ Mountain Bike Trail
◆ Recreational & Mountain Bike Trails

Busch Memorial Conservation Area

Trail Uses	🚲 🏃
Vicinity	Weldon Spring
Trail Length	3.2 miles
Surface	Natural, groomed
County	St. Charles

Trail Notes   The August A. Busch Memorial Conservation Area is a 7,000 acre wildlife preserve offering a diverse landscape with easy trails that explore a wide variety of habitats. This old ammo production site is under the Dept. of Conservation management, and is perhaps the best place in the St. Louis area to admire Missouri's plants and animals. Lakes dot the landscape, ranging from tiny ponds to the 182 acre Lake 33.

The trail's effort level is easy, following a combination of old roads from the area's military days and more recent double-tracks. It's smooth surface and gentle grades make it a perfect trail for the novice and for family outings. The trail's two loops pass through forests and food plots, and along a dam bordering Lake 33. The area is home to ducks, geese, songbirds, deer, and osprey.

There is also a 8.7 mile driving tour of the Busch Area, and 6 foot trails, ranging in length from .2 to the .7 mile Fallen Oak Nature Trail. Fallen Oak Nature Trail is asphalt paved and is located at the picnic area near the park headquarters.

Getting There   From St. Louis go west on Hwy 40/61 to Hwy 94, then left for a mile to Hwy D and the entrance to the Wildlife Area and the Visitor Center. The trailhead is off B Road just south of Lake 33.

Contact
August A. Busch Wildlife Area
515-441-4554
2360 Hwy. D
St. Charles, MO 63304

TRAIL LEGEND	
———	Trail-Biking/Multi
·············	Hiking only Trail
• • • • • • • •	Hiking - Multi Use
▪▪▪▪▪▪▪▪	Snowmobiling only
==========	Planned Trail
▬ ▬ ▬ ▬	Alternate Trail
———	Road/Highway
+++++++++++	Railroad Tracks

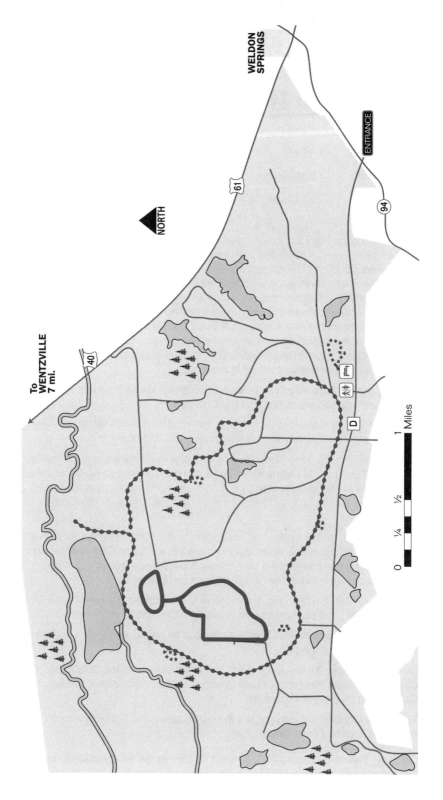

WELDON
SPRINGS

ENTRANCE

NORTH

To
WENTZVILLE
7 mi.

61

94

40

D

0   ¼   ½   1   Miles

Castlewood State Park

Trail Uses	
Vicinity	Ballwin
Trail Length	15.5
Surface	Natural, groomed
County	St. Louis

Trail Notes   The 1,779 acre Castlewood State Park provides a wide variety of natural habitats, including forests, hills, flood plain, gravel bars and the Meramec River. It straddles both sides of the Meramec River, and is part of the Meramec River Recreation Area, which stretches from Meramec State Park to the river's confluence with the Mississippi River south of St. Louis. A feature of the park is the majestic white limestone bluffs that tower above the Meramec River. From the early to mid 1900's, Castlewood served as a premiere resort of the many thousands of St. Louisans who would flock there on weekends for canoeing, dancing and sunning along the river beaches. Still existing is the grand staircase, which guided visitors to the several resort hotels and summer cabins located in the area.

The trail system is off-road single track. The terrain varies from flat bottomland to steep hill climbs and ridge riding.

Grotpeter Trail, 3 miles long, is hilly and technical as it winds along the park's wooded uplands. You can access it from near the first picnic shelter.

River Scene Trail, a 3 mile loop, begins opposite the entrance road to the first picnic shelter. The trail climbs to the bluffs along the Meramec River, and then descends to the flood plain along the river's edge and back to the start point. This trail has some short, technical sections, but the surface is mostly dirt and fairly flat.

Stinging Nettle Trail, 3 miles long, circles the bottomland forest adjacent to the river. The difficulty level is easy, but there are several large depressions with many ups and downs resulting from gravel dredging operations years ago. The trail was named after the Stinging Nettle plants that line it.

Cedar Bluff Trail, 2 miles long, begins near the end of the Stinging Nettle Trail loop. This trail provides some great views from the hilltops you'll ride.

The 1.5 mile Long Wolf Trail is hilly, rocky and technical. It trails through the wooded uplands of the park.

Castlewood Loop, 3 miles long, is flat and takes you along the bottomland of Castlewood State Park and Lincoln Beach. It provides some great views of Castlewood Bluff across the river.

The 7 mile Chubb Trail also passes through Castlewood State Park as it continues west to Tyson County Park.

Getting There   From I-270, go west on Hwy 40/64 for 9.5 miles to the Long Road exit. Turn left onto Long Road and go one mile to Wild Horse

Creek Road. Turn Right onto Wild Horse Creek Road and continue three miles to the Hwy 109 stop sign. Turn left and go less than a mile to Route BA. Turn right and continue for 1.5 miles to the park entrance.

If you're coming from I-44, exit at Hwy 141, Meramec State Road, and go north (right). Turn left onto Big Bend, which turns into Oak Street. Turn left at Ries Road. Go over the hill and turn left at the Castlewood Sign.

Contact   Castlewood State Park   636-227-4433
1401 Kiefer Creek Road
Ballwin, MO 63021

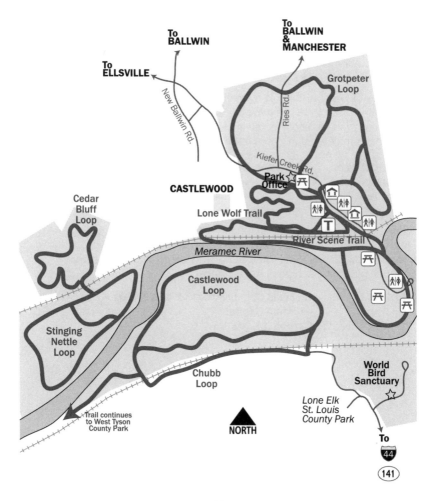

Chubb Trail

Trail Uses	🚵 🚶
Vicinity	St. Louis
Trail Length	7 miles
Surface	Gravel, dirt
County	St. Louis

Trail Notes   This 7 mile gravel and dirt trail runs for 7 miles from West Tyson County Park, through Castlewood State Park, to Lone Elk Park in St. Louis County. Effort level is moderate to difficult. The terrain is rocky and often slippery. It has some very challenging hills and fast stretches. Be aware of the drop-offs. This is a well maintained single-track for most of the trail, with some double-track in the eastern sections. It is probably the most popular mountain bike trail in the St. Louis area.

From the Tyson Trailhead, the first three miles are mostly steep climbs, long descents, and fast stretches. The next three miles are flat, following the riverbank. Another mile of uphill fire roads then brings you to Lone Elk Park at the other end. You will experience some great views along the ride.

The Lone Elk Park is home to a small herd of bison and elk, with picnic areas and a lake. Tyson Park has camping, water, and picnic facilities. The river is sometimes prone to flooding, putting some of the trail under water. Park hours are from 8 am (7 am during summers) to a half hour past sunset.

Getting There   The Chubb Trail is located about 15 miles southwest of St. Louis. From St. Louis, take I-44 west, getting off at Lewis Road, Exit 265. Enter West Tyson Park, and go up a hill to the end of the road and park. The trailheads are on the right of the entrance.

Alternately you can go to the other end of the Chubb Trail by exiting I-44 at Hwy 141 (Meramec Road). Turn west (right) on the Outer Road, and follow it to Lone Elk County Park. The Chubb Trailhead is the fire road before the Lone Elk gates on the right of the entrance.

Contact	St. Louis County Parks 314-822-9904
	41 South Central
	Clayton, MO 63105

St. Louis Metropolitan Area – Missouri

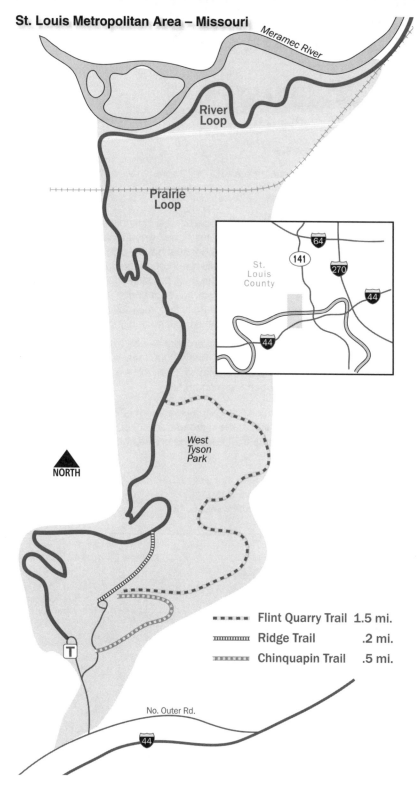

Meramec River

River Loop

Prairie Loop

St. Louis County

West Tyson Park

NORTH

Flint Quarry Trail 1.5 mi.
Ridge Trail .2 mi.
Chinquapin Trail .5 mi.

No. Outer Rd.

Cliff Cave Park Trails

Trail Uses	🚲 🚶 🎧
Vicinity	St. Louis
Trail Length	5 miles
Surface	Natural, groomed
County	St. Louis

Trail Notes   Cliff Cave Park is located on a sinkhole plateau above the Mississippi River, with nearly 200 acres of oak woodlands. Tall northern red oaks and white oaks dominate. This unusual natural and geologic feature is well worth your visit. The series of trails run through the upland woodlands, an old field and a degraded savanna. The trails are singletrack and fire roads. Effort level would be mostly moderate. You will experience a variety of steep hills, logs, and rocky areas. Some of the trails become muddy after heavy rains. There are restrooms and picnic tables, but no drinking water facilities.

Cliff Cave itself is a generally shallow cavern that can be explored by qualified individuals and groups for a distance of nearly 2000 feet. You must have a reservation and permit if you desire to explore. Call 3214-615-4FUN. Permits are issued for the hours between 8 am and 5 pm.

Getting There   Go south on Telegraph Road from I-270, then east on Cliff Cave Road to the dead end at the railroad tracks. You'll have to climb up the paved road to get to the two trailheads, one on the right and the other on the left, near the top of the hill.

Contact   Cliff Cave County Park   314-615-4386
                 806 Cliff Cave Road
                 St. Louis County, MO 63129

St. Louis Metropolitan Area – Missouri

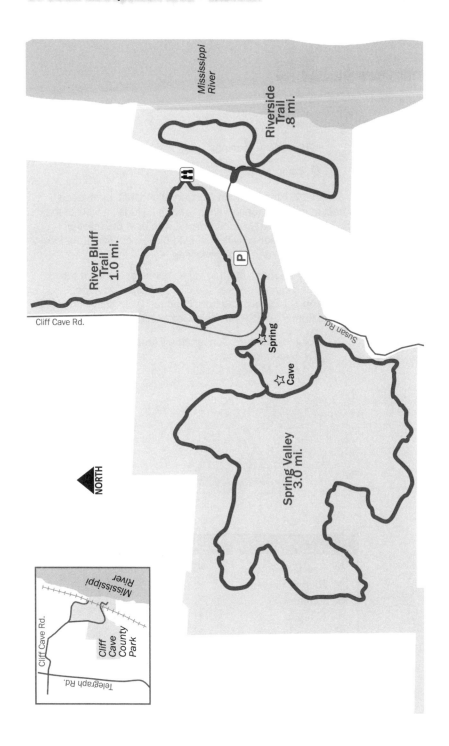

25

Columbia Bottom Conservation Area

Trail Uses   🚲 🏃

Vicinity	St. Charles
Trail Length	5 miles
Surface	Limestone screenings
County	St. Louis

Trail Notes   In 1997 the Missouri Conservation Dept. purchased this 4,318 acre tract to create a conservation area. It includes a view of the confluence of the Mississippi and Missouri rivers, with over 6.5 miles of river frontage. The more popular activities include bicycling, hiking, outdoor photography, fishing, hunting, and wildlife viewing.

Bicycles are allowed only on roads open to vehicles and designated trails, and are not permitted on service roads or the River's Edge Trail. The Conservation Area is open to public use from 6 am to 10 pm daily from April 1 to September 30 and from 6 am to 7 pm from October 1 to March 31.

Contact   Columbia Bottom Conservation Area   314-877-6014
               801 Strodtman Road
               St. Louis, Missouri 63188

SYMBOL LEGEND	
🏖 Beach/Swimming	MF Multi-Facilities
🚲 Bicycle Repair	P Parking
🏠 Cabin	🞡 Picnic
△ Camping	🛡 Ranger Station
🛶 Canoe Launch	🚻 Restrooms
➕ First Aid	⌂ Shelter
ⓐ Food	T Trailhead
GC Golf Course	🏛 Visitor Center
? Information	🜊 Water
🛏 Lodging	👁 Overlook/ Observation

St. Louis Metropolitan Area – Missouri

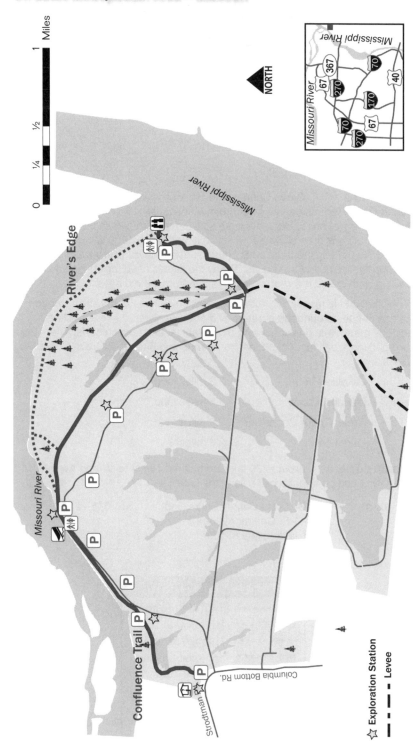

Creve Coeur Memorial Park

Trail Uses	
Vicinity	Creve Coeur
Trail Length	12 miles
Surface	Asphalt
County	St. Louis

Trail Notes   Creve Coeur is French for "broken heart". According to legend an Indian maiden was heart-broken because a French trapper she loved, never returned. Her tears were said to form the lake in the shape of a heart, and she then drowned herself in it. In the late 1800's, St. Louisans visited the park by the thousands on hot summer days. There was even an amusement park and two hotels. Today the lake is used for sailing and some fishing, with only a few remnants remaining from the old days.

The bike path is mostly flat, with only a few small rises and a short wooden bridge. It goes around the northern end of Creve Coeur Lake. Facilities include restrooms, drinking water, picnic tables, and tennis courts. There are two parking areas located off Marine Avenue and one off of Creve Coeur Mill Road.

Lakeview Loop	3.7 miles long
Meadows Loop	2.8 miles long
Creve Coeur Connector	2.8 miles long
Lake Loop	2.6 miles

Getting There   From I-270 take Dorsett road west to Marine Avenue. Turn right and go about a half mile to the lake.

Contact   St. Louis County Parks Dept.   314-615-7275
41 S. Central Avenue
Clayton, MO 63105

TRAIL LEGEND	
————	Trail-Biking/Multi
··············	Hiking only Trail
••••••••••	Hiking - Multi Use
▪▪▪▪▪▪▪▪	Snowmobiling only
==========	Planned Trail
▬ ▬ ▬ ▬ ▬	Alternate Trail
————	Road/Highway
++++++++++	Railroad Tracks

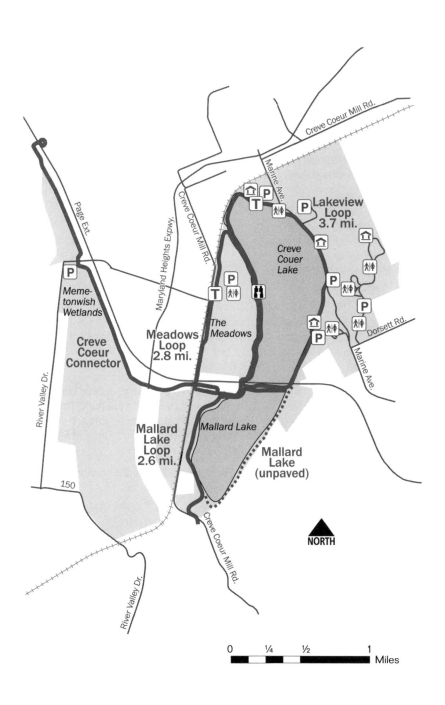

Creve Coeur Mill Rd.

Marine Ave.

Page Ext.

Creve Coeur Mill Rd.

Maryland Heights Expwy.

Lakeview Loop 3.7 mi.

Creve Couer Lake

Meme-tonwish Wetlands

Creve Coeur Connector

Meadows Loop 2.8 mi.

The Meadows

River Valley Dr.

Dorsett Rd.

Marine Ave.

Mallard Lake Loop 2.6 mi.

Mallard Lake

Mallard Lake (unpaved)

150

NORTH

Creve Coeur Mill Rd.

River Valley Dr.

| 0 | ¼ | ½ | 1 |

Miles

Forest Park Bike Path

Trail Uses	🚲 🚶 🎧
Vicinity	St. Louis
Trail Length	8.5 miles
Surface	Paved

Trail Notes   Forest Park is a 1,300 acre city park in midtown St. Louis. It was dedicated in 1876 and served as the focal point of the 1904 World's Fair. Several buildings still remain today, including the Art Museum, the Bird Cage, and the Grand Basin.

Highlights include:
* The #1 zoo in the United States according to Zagat's 2004 Guide
* First national memorial to Thomas Jefferson
* American oldest and largest outdoor musical theatre, the Muny Opera
* World's Fair Pavilion
* Art Museum
* Planetarium
* History Museum

The paved path is very popular, attracting more than 12 million visitors a year. There is an Outer loop of some 7 miles and an Inner loop of 1.5 miles. Restrooms, drinking fountains, and picnic areas are located throughout the park.

Getting There   There are several entrances into the park. You can take Hwy 64/40 to Kingshighway Blvd. North, then turn left into the park. There are also entrances off Hampton, Lindell and Skinker. Parking lots are located around the park, including the History Museum, the Art Museum, the Muny, and Steinberg Rink.

Contact	City of St. Louis Parks Recreation and Forestry
	314-289-5300
	5600 Clayton Avenue
	St. Louis, MO 63110

St. Louis Metropolitan Area – Missouri

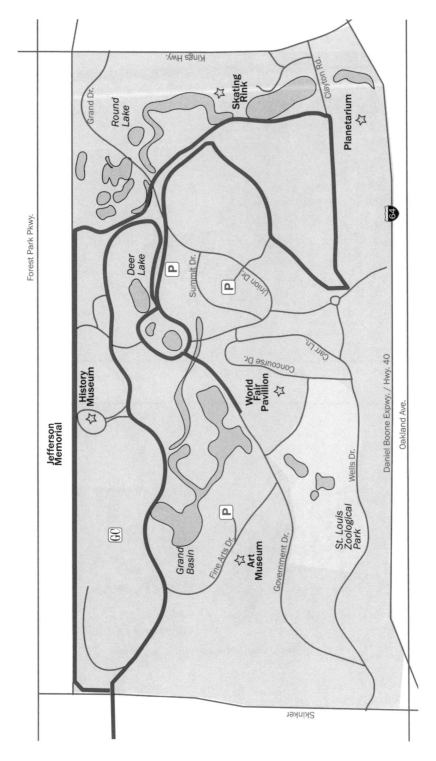

Youngster about to ride the Forest Park Bike Path

A stop along the Forest Park Bike Path

All photos courtesy of Trailnet, Inc.

Young cyclists posing on he Forest Park Bike Path St. Louis Zoo entrance

Riding Grant's Trail

Grant's Trail

Trail Uses	

Trail Uses

Vicinity   St. Louis

Trail Length   6 miles

Surface   Asphalt

County   St. Louis

Trail Notes   This popular trail is located in south St. Louis County. The first six miles of the trail from the Orlando Garden Trailhead to Pardee Road are paved. There is another two miles ending at Hwy 44 that is surfaced with rough gravel. The trail travels along the Gravois Creek and was built along a section of the old Missouri Pacific railroad right-of-way in 1997. The trail setting features wetlands, a pond, bird wildlife, and an ecological education facility. It is open year round from dawn to dusk.

Grant's Trail is named after Ulysses S. Grant, former president and military general, who owned the land in the surrounding area. Drinking water is available at the Trailnet office located at Reavis Barracks Road, and restrooms can be found across from the office. More than 100,000 visitors a year use the trail.

Getting There   Eastern Trailhead – Take the Reavis Barrack Road exit off I-55 and go east. At Union Road, turn north (left), and then right onto Hoffmeister just before Union Avenue goes over I-55. Take Hoffmeister to the Orlando Gardens Banquet Center and park on the lower parking lot.

Western Trailhead – Take the Tesson Ferry Road exit off I-270 and go north for 2 miles. Turn left onto Musick Road, and then right onto Tesshire Road after about 100 feet. You can park adjacent to Hill Behan Lumber by the trail.

Contact   St. Louis County Parks   314-615-7275
               41 S. Clayton Avenue
               Clayton, MO 63165

Riding Grant's Trail. Photo courtesy of Trailnet, Inc.

St. Louis Metropolitan Area – Missouri

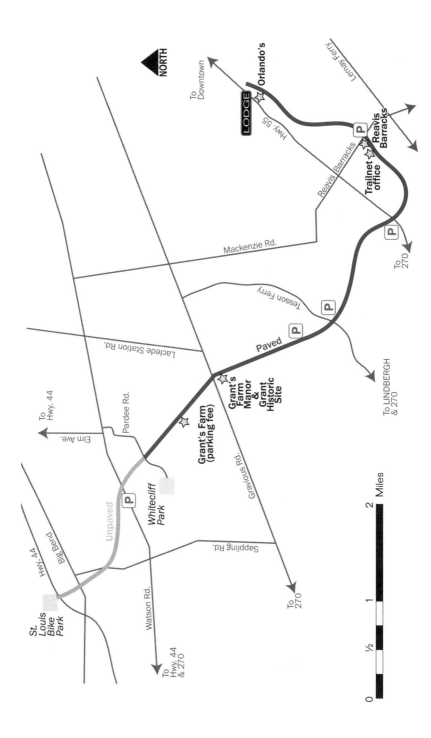

Greenfelder County Park

Trail Uses	🚴 🏃 ⛺
Vicinity	Eureka
Trail Length	6.5 miles
Surface	Natural, groomed
County	St. Louis

Trail Notes   The 1,760 acre Greensfelder County Park is named after A. P. Greensfleder, a environmentalist and open space supporter, who once owned the land. Facilities include drinking water, camping, and a nature learning center. The park is located in western St. Louis County near Six Flags. Also nearby is the Shaw Arboretum, which has hiking and walking trails, but no trails open to biking.

This is probably one of the most challenging spots to ride in Missouri. The trails are technical single track, with steep climbs and descents over large rocks and sometimes muddy areas. Only the 2.5 mile DeClue and the 4 mile Dogwoods Trails are open for mountain biking. Overall effort level is moderate. Greensfelder is a popular park for horseback riding, hiking and cycling. Detailed maps are available at the Visitor Center.

Getting There   Take I-44 west from St. Louis to the Six flags/Allenton exit, just west of Eureka. Take Allenton Road north for 2 miles to the park entrance, and park at the Visitor Center.

Contact   St. Louis County Parks   314-615-7275
41 South Central
Clayton, MO 63105

AREA LEGEND	
	City, Town
	Parks, Preserves
▢	Waterway
	Marsh/Wetland
▬▬▬	Mileage Scale
★	Points of Interest
– –	County/State
🌲	Forest/Woods

TRAIL LEGEND	
▬▬▬▬▬	Trail-Biking/Multi
·············	Hiking only Trail
••••••••••	Hiking - Multi Use
▬▬▬▬▬	Snowmobiling only
==========	Planned Trail
▬ ▬ ▬ ▬	Alternate Trail
▬▬▬▬▬	Road/Highway
+++++++++++	Railroad Tracks

St. Louis Metropolitan Area – Missouri

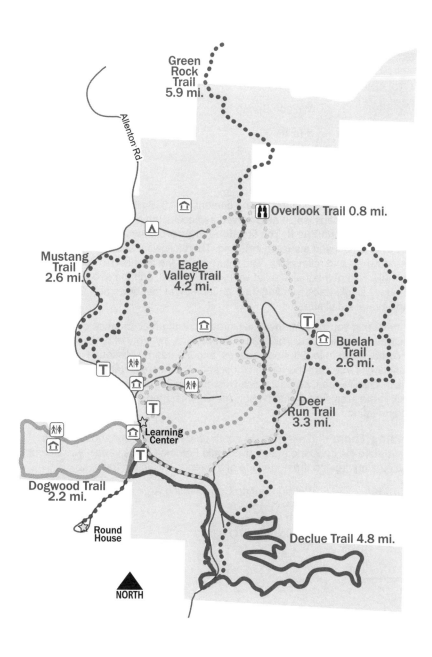

Lost Valley Trail
(Weldon Spring Conservation Area)

Trail Uses

Vicinity   Weldon Spring

Trail Length   8 miles

Surface   Dirt

County   St. Charles

Trail Notes   Weldon Spring comprises 7,356 acres. The 8 mile loop uses old farm roads which also served as access to ammunition stockpiles there during World War II. The first three miles are fairly easy, lined with small hills and valleys and a stream crossing. Then follows a short climb followed by a downhill and rolling hills. The return trip to the trailhead is generally downhill. Half of the trail is a flat wide country road, and the second half is generally single track, winding through forest and meadows and along ridges and several small streams.

In the spring you'll find many small streams, with an abundance of wildflowers decorating the hillsides. The area also supports a variety of bird species, with its combination of forest, open spaces, and the nearby Missouri River habitat. Many apple trees dot the green landscape. The nearest water source is the Busch Wildlife Area, some 2 miles west of Hwy 94 and Hwy D. Poison ivy is thick in the area. The Conservation Area is managed by the Missouri Dept. of Conservation.

Getting There   Take Hwy 94 south past Hwy 40/64 for about 5 miles. Just before the one-lane bridge over Little Femme Osage Creek, you'll come to a parking area on the north side of the road. This is the trailhead.

Contact   Weldon Spring Conservation Area
                  636-441-4554
                  2340 Highway D
                  St. Charles, MO 63303

AREA LEGEND	
	City, Town
	Parks, Preserves
	Waterway
	Marsh/Wetland
	Mileage Scale
★	Points of Interest
– –	County/State
	Forest/Woods

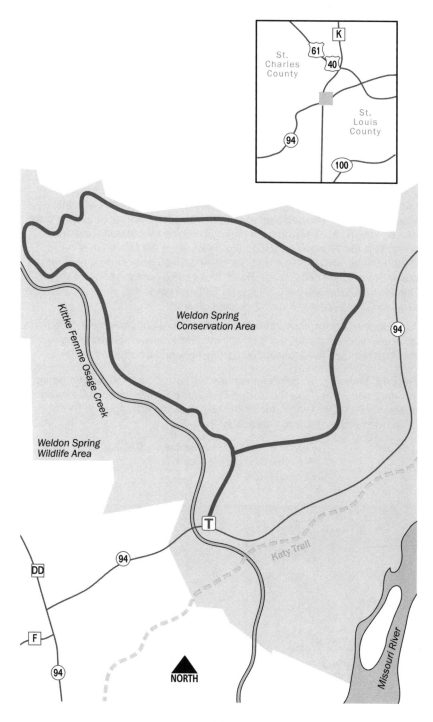

Meramec Greenway & Fenton City Park

Trail Uses	
Vicinity	Fenton
Trail Length	5.5 miles
Surface	Paved
County	St. Louis

Trail Notes   The Meramec Greenway spans the majority of the southern boundary of St. Louis County. It follows the Meramec River for approximately 50 river miles west to the Meramec's confluence with the Mississippi River. The trail begins in Fenton City Park where it travels around a loop in the park, then exists the park, crosses by Henderson Field and Larkin Williams Road. It continues southeast along the Meramec River to Mound Street, where the paved bike trail ends. You can continue east on Water Street to the Old Gravois Road, cross going northeast. Turn east on Opps Lane just before the Old Gravois Bridge. Turn to the left by the trail sign to get to George Winter Park where the ride ends.

As mentioned above, a short section is on road without a bike lane. There are a few hills, but the terrain is mostly flat. Facilities such as restrooms and drinking water are available in Fenton City Park and George Winter Park.

Getting There   To get to Fenton from St. Louis, take I-44 west crossing the Meramec River. Take the Soccer Park/North Highway exit, and turn right on Soccer Park Drive. At Yarnell turn right, and then right again at Sweaney Drive, which takes you into Fenton City Park.

Contact	Fenton Parks and Recreation 636-343-0067
	645 New Smitzer Mill Road
	Fenton, MO 63026

St. Louis Metropolitan Area – Missouri

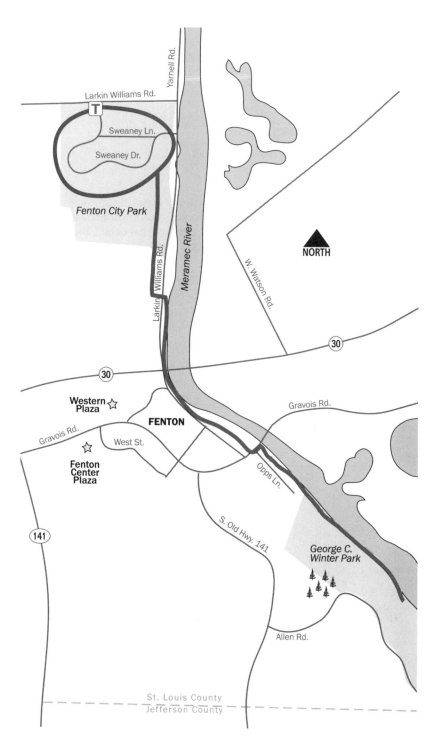

Yarnell Rd.

Larkin Williams Rd.

T

Sweaney Ln.

Sweaney Dr.

Fenton City Park

Larkin Williams Rd.

Meramec River

W. Watson Rd.

NORTH

30

30

Western Plaza

Gravois Rd.

FENTON

Gravois Rd.

West St.

Opps Ln.

Fenton Center Plaza

S. Old Hwy. 141

141

George C. Winter Park

Allen Rd.

St. Louis County
Jefferson County

Queeny County Park

Trail Uses	
Vicinity	Ballwin
Trail Length	28 miles
Surface	Paved, gravel roads, dirt
County	St. Louis

Trail Notes   Queeny Park has 7.8 miles of mountain bike trails, 1.5 miles of which are paved. In addition there is a 20 mile horse and mountain bike trail loop in the more hilly and wooded section of the park. Other than the paved & gravel roads, the effort level is moderate. The horseback trail includes jumps, fences, and water area.

Facilities at this 569 acre park include a parking lot, rest rooms, and a recreation complex with a seasonal indoor ice rink and outdoor roller hockey rink. Hour long hayrides are available for rental. The park provides habitat for eagles, hawks, turkey, quail, herons, waterfowl, and shorebirds. Deer, rabbits and squirrels are quite common.

Getting There   From I-270, go west on Manchester Road, then right on Weidmann Road to the park entrance.

Contact	Queeny County Park	636-391-0900
	550 Weidman Road	
	Ballwin, MO 63011	

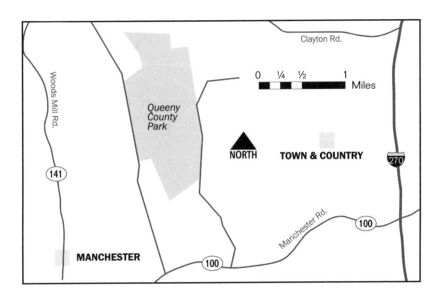

St. Louis Metropolitan Area – Missouri

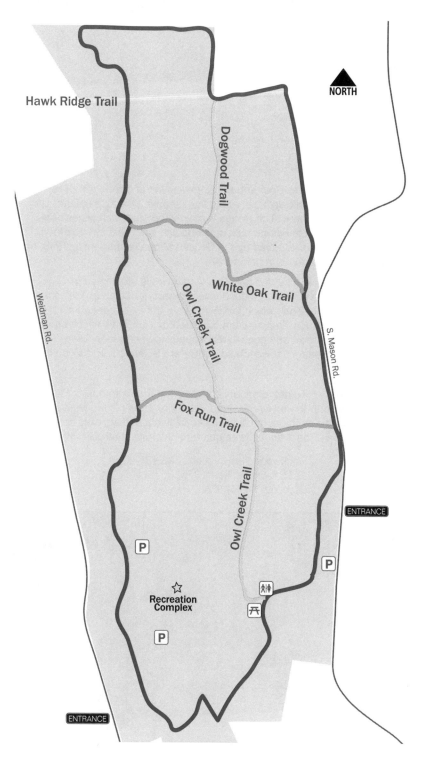

NORTH

Hawk Ridge Trail

Dogwood Trail

White Oak Trail

Owl Creek Trail

Weidman Rd.

S. Mason Rd.

Fox Run Trail

Owl Creek Trail

ENTRANCE

P

P

☆ Recreation Complex

P

ENTRANCE

Rockwood Range Conservation Area

Trail Uses	🚵 🚶
Vicinity	Glencoe
Trail Length	6 miles
Surface	Natural, groomed
County	St. Louis

Trail Notes   The Rockwoods Range lies in the Ozark border region. Ozark like hills and hollows occur along the streams, with many plants and animals overlapping here. The Range is mostly forested, with occasional prairies and glades. Limestone rock outcrops and sinkholes are common. The 1,388 acre range was acquired by the Conservation Department in 1943, and is open from sunrise to hour after sunset.

The shared mountain bike and horseback riding trails are limited to designated trails only. They are the 3 miles Round House Loop Trail, the 0.6 mile Fox Creek Spur Trail, which leads you from the Fox Creek parking lot to the Round House Loop Trail, and the 3.5 mile Fox Run Trail, which begins at the Fox Run parking lot and goes to the Round House memorial site. Scenic overlooks, tree plantations, woodland wildlife are features found along the trails.

Getting There   To get to the area, exit I-44 at the Allenton/Six Flags exit and travel north to Fox Creek Road. Take Fox Creek Road west to the parking lot located on the south side. There is also a parking area on the east side of Fox Creek Road, about three quarters of a mile south of Hwy 100.

Contact	Rockwood Reservation 636-468-2236
	2751 Glencoe Road
	Glencoe, MO 63038

St. Louis Metropolitan Area – Missouri

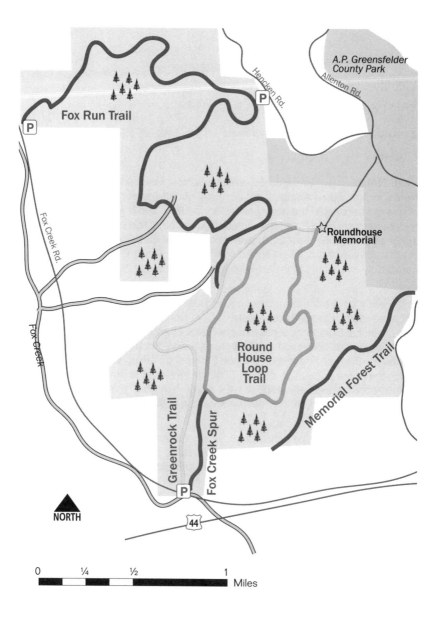

A.P. Greensfelder County Park

Hencken Rd.

Allenton Rd.

P

P

Fox Run Trail

P

Fox Creek Rd.

☆ Roundhouse Memorial

Fox Creek

Round House Loop Trail

Greenrock Trail

Fox Creek Spur

Memorial Forest Trail

▲
NORTH

P

44

0	¼	½	1

Miles

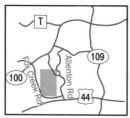

T

109

100

Allenton Rd.

Fox Creek Rd.

44

Route 66 State Park

Trail Uses	🚴 🏃 🎧
Vicinity	Eureka
Trail Length	7 miles
Surface	Paved, aggregate
County	St. Louis

Trail Notes   Highway 66, America's most famous highway, running from Chicago to Los Angeles, got its name when Midwest business leaders convened to christen the east-west artery in 1926. The leaders had wanted it to be named Hwy 60, but that number was already taken, so someone suggested Hwy 66. Missouri's newest park, Route 66 State Park is located on 419 acres of the once-poisoned community of Times Beach, which was completely evacuated in the early seventies because of high concentrations of dioxin.

In the early 1970's the town hired hauler Russell Bliss to oil the town's unpaved roads. Bliss sprayed waste oil from Northeastern Pharmaceutical and Chemical Company, a producer of Agent Orange, over a period of four years. As horses continued to die at area stables, the owners contacted the Center for Disease Prevention and the EPA began taking samples in 1982. In 1985, the entire population of over 2,000 was evacuated, and the town was disincorporated. Between 1996 & 1997 the government removed 265,000 tons of contaminated debris from the area at a cost of $110 million to make the land safe again.

The park's interpretive center displays a fine collection of memorabilia donated by the Route 66 Association of Missouri. There's also an interesting presentation of the history of Times Beach, and excellent opportunities to picnic or study nature.

Getting There   The park is approximately 25 miles from I-70/I-270. Travel I-270 south to I-44 west to Exit 266/Lewis Road. Follow the road to the right and then curve to the left. Continue past the West Tyson County Park entrance to the stop sign at Lewis Road. After crossing Lewis Road, you will come to the visitor center on your left. Continue across the bridge to enter the park grounds.

Contact	Route 66 State Park 636-938-7198
	97 North Other Road
	Eureka, MO 63026

St. Louis Metropolitan Area – Missouri

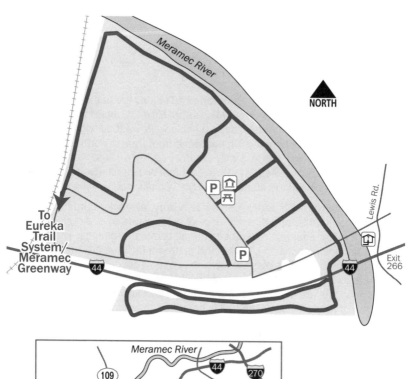

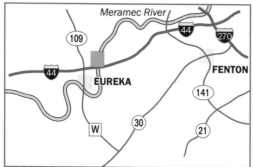

St. Louis Riverfront Trail

Trail Uses	🚵 🏃 🛼
Vicinity	St. Louis
Trail Length	12 miles
Surface	Asphalt

Trail Notes   The St. Louis Riverfront Trail, as the name implies, travels alongside the shores of the Mississippi River. It begins at Lenore K. Sullivan and Biddle Streets at the old Laclede Power building near the Gateway Arch and continues north past Riverfront Park in north St. Louis, to the old Chain of Rocks Bridge, a mile south of I-270. In 1999, the Chain of Rocks Bridge was converted to a 1 mile, 24 foot wide multi-use recreational trail, and is now part of the 40 miles riverside Confluence Greenway project.

The trail passes through parts of St. Louis history, along the borders of old St. Louis neighborhoods, and through fields of diverse wildlife and native plants. Bald Eagles, fox, squirrels and rabbits are all common sightings. The trail can become flooded on occasion. Water and restroom facilities are available at the Coast Guard Building rest area, which is open Tuesday through Friday from 7 am to 7 pm, and Saturday and Sunday from 9 am to 5 pm. Restrooms and a parking lot are also accessible at North Riverview Park, just past the Old Chain of Rocks Bridge. The trail is open from 6 am to 10 pm.

Getting There   Downtown St. Louis – Lenore K. Sullivan and Biddle Streets at the old Laclede Power building.

From North County – take I-270 to Riverview Drive South. The north trailhead is at the south end of the park, at the second parking area, about 2.8 miles from I-270.

Contact	Trailnet, Inc.	314-416-9930
	3900 Reavis Barracks	
	St. Louis, MO 63125	

Riding the St. Louis Riverfront Trail   *Photo courtesy of Trailnet, Inc.*

St. Louis Metropolitan Area – Missouri

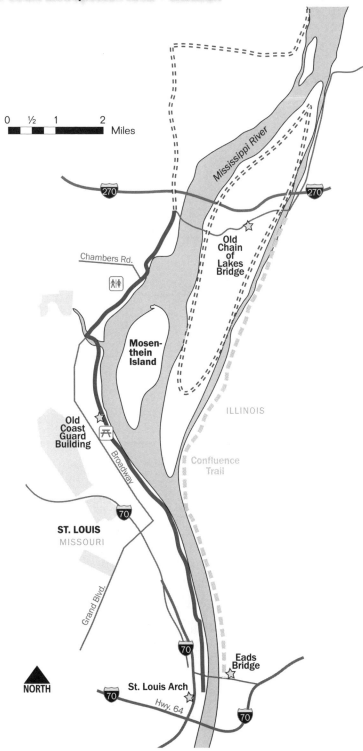

0   ½   1   2   Miles

Mississippi River

270   270

Old Chain of Lakes Bridge

Chambers Rd.

Mosen-thein Island

ILLINOIS

Old Coast Guard Building

Broadway

Confluence Trail

70

ST. LOUIS
MISSOURI

Grand Blvd.

70

Eads Bridge

NORTH

70   St. Louis Arch

Hwy. 64   70

Riding the St. Louis Riverfront Trail

St. Louis Metropolitan Area – Missouri

All photos courtesy of Trailnet, Inc.

Madison County Trails 🚲 🛼 🏃

Bluff Trail
Trail Length 2 miles   **Surface** Paved
Location & Setting A 2 mile, asphalt trail connecting the Nature
Trail at the Southern Illinois University campus to the south and the on-road
bikeway on New Poag Road to the north. Parking is available on Bluff Road
at the SIUE Delyte Morris trail, at Korte Stadium and at St. Paul's Church of
Christ in Edwardsville.

Confluence Trail
Trail Length 16 miles   **Surface** Asphalt and Oil & Chip
Location & Setting The Confluence Trail is a 16 mile trail connecting Alton
to Granite City, mainly along the Mississippi River levee. The surface is a
combination of asphalt and oil and chip. The ride provides spectacular views
of the Mississippi River, and popular stops such as the Lock & Dam 26 Visitor
Center in East Alton and the Lewis & Clark Interpretive Center in Hartford.
It also connects Illinois to Missouri over the historic Chain of Rock Bridge.
Parking is available at Russell Commons Park in Alton, the Lock & Dam 26
Visitor Center, the Lewis & Clark Interpretive Center in Hartford, and both the
Illinois and Missouri side of the Chain of Rock Bridge.

Delyte Morris Trail
Trail Length 2.8 miles   **Surface** Paved
Location & Setting This path proceeds from the courthouse in
Edwardsville to Bluff Road on the western edge of the Southern Illinois
University campus. From Edwardsville the trail continues down a small
valley and through some heavily wooded area. Sections are rugged with hilly
terrain. Once out of the woods, it follows an old railroad right-of-way through
prairie areas. Parking is available at the Cougar Lake recreation area.

Glen Carbon Heritage Trail
Trail Length 11 miles   **Surface** Asphalt and crushed stone
Location & Setting The trail follows the old Illinois Central RR route from
Hwy 255, through Glen Carbon, a natural passage in the bluffs, and onto
restored prairies on top of the bluffs. The surface is asphalt and merimac
gravel. Parking, restroom and picnic facilities can be found in Miner Park, a
few blocks off the trail in Glen Carbon. Along the trail are several historical
markers and 8 timber trestle bridges. The Silver Creek Railroad trestle is 340
feet long. Glen Carbon is located in Madison County by the confluence of
Hwy 70, 55, 270 and 255. A good trail starting off point is from behind the fire
station in Glen Carbon or from Miner Park.

Nature Trail
Trail Length 12 miles   **Surface** Asphalt
Location & Setting The Nature Trail is built along the old Illinois Terminal
Railroad line. It begins at Hwy 159 and Longfellow Rd in Edwardsville near
the Lewis & Clark Community College N.O. Nelson campus, continuing
through the Southern Illinois University Edwardsville campus, and then
southwest to Lake Dr in Pontoon Beach. Parking is available at the St. Paul
United Church of Christ at Longfellow Rd and Nelson Ave, at Longfellow Rd
at Hwy 159 in Edwardsville, and at Revelle Ln in Pontoon Beach.

Nickel Plate Trail

Trail Length 4.6 miles   **Surface** Crushed limestone

Location & Setting The 4.6 mile Nickel Plate Trail is built along a section of the New York, Toledo, St. Louis Railroad line nicknamed the "Nickel Plate." It connects the Nature Trail to the west edge of the Glen Carbon Heritage Trail. The surface is crushed limestone. It begins at Hwy 159 and Longfellow Road in Edwardsville and extends south to the Glen Carbon Heritage Trail at Main Street in Glen Carbon.

Parking is available at Longfellow Road at Nelson Avenue, at Longfellow Road at Hwy 159 adjacent to the LCCC N.O. Nelson campus in Edwardsville, and at Main Street in Glen Carbon behind the ball field.

Quercus Grove Trail

Trail Length 3 miles   **Surface** Asphalt

Location & Setting The Quercus Grove Trail is a 3 mile asphalt trail beginning at the Nickel Plate Trail, at the intersection of Schwarz and Springer Streets in downtown Edwardsville, and extending northeast along Hwy 157 to Hazel Road in rural Edwardsville where it ends.

Parking is available in Edwardsville at the Park and Ride Lot for the Madison County Transit Edwardsville Station.

Schoolhouse Trail

Trail Length 11.5 miles   **Surface** Asphalt

Location & Setting The Schoolhouse Trail connects the communities of Collinsville, Maryville, Troy, Granite City and Pontoon Beach. The surface is asphalt. The trail begins at the intersection of Hwy 162 and Edwardsville/Troy Road in Troy and extends past Drost Park in Maryville to Horseshoe Lake State Park in Granite City. There is an on-road bikeway just east of I-255 to the Gateway Convention Center.

Parking is available at Horseshoe Lake State Park in Granite City, at Gateway Convention Center in Collinsville, at Drost Park in Maryville, and at Hwy 162 at Edwardsville/Troy Road in Troy.

Watershed Trail

Trail Length 5 miles   **Surface** Asphalt

Location & Setting The 5 mile Watershed Trail is built along abandoned rail corridor between West Union Street in Edwardsville and northwest to the Watershed Nature Center and Wanda Road in Roxana. There is a 2 mile on-road connection linking the trail to New Poag Road. The trail surface is asphalt.

There is parking on Russell Road and at the Watershed Nature Center on Tower Avenue adjacent to the N.O. Nelson Elementary School in Edwardsville.

Under development is a 7 mile trail connector between the Schoolhouse Trail near Troy to the to the Glen Carbon Heritage Trail, the Nickel Plat Trail, the Nature Trail, the Delyte W. Morris Trail and the Watershed Trail in Edwardsville.

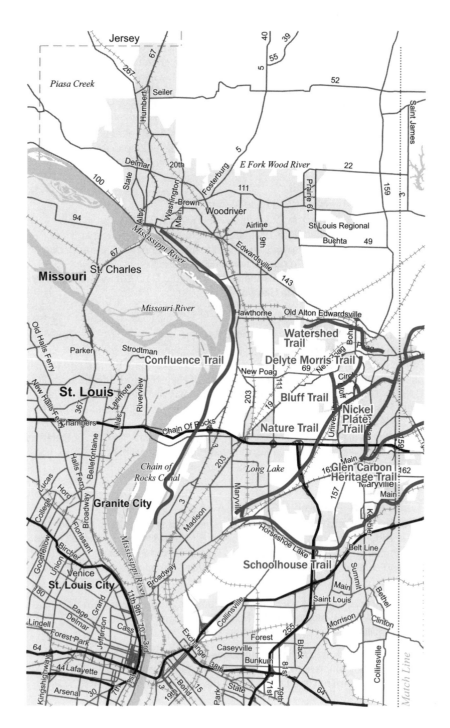

St. Louis Metropolitan Area – Illinois

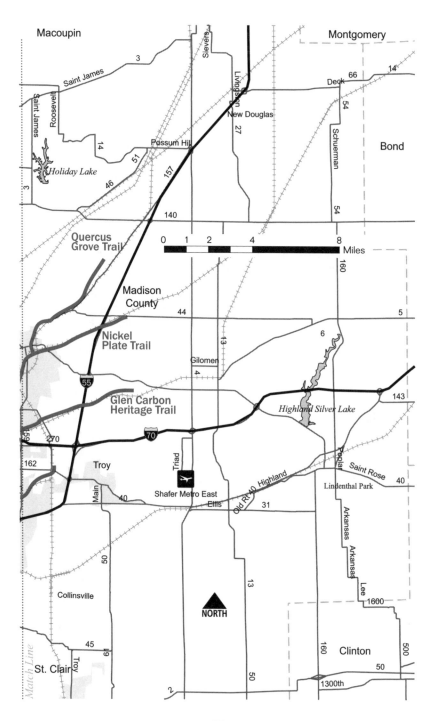

Vadalabene Bike Trail

Trail Uses	🚴 🚶
Vicinity	Alton, Grafton
Trail Length	19 miles
Surface	Paved
Counties	Madison & Jersey, Illinois

Trail Notes   This path follows Route 100 between Alton, through Grafton and to Pere Marquette State Park. The bikeway is bordered by towering limestone cliffs to the north and the Mississippi River to the south, and is a recreational destination for bicycle enthusiast.

The northern section follows the wide paved shoulders of the McAdams Parkway to Grafton. The southern section is a separate paved path built on an abandoned railroad line at the base of the bluffs. There are parking areas along and at each end of the bikeway. Pause to visit the historic town of Grafton and Elsah with their antique shops.

Getting There   From Missouri, take Hwy 67/367 north through West Alton and across the Mississippi River. Upon crossing the river turn left onto Hwy 100 to the trailhead, a short distance further on the right side of the road.

Contact	Illinois Dept. of Transportation 618-346-3100

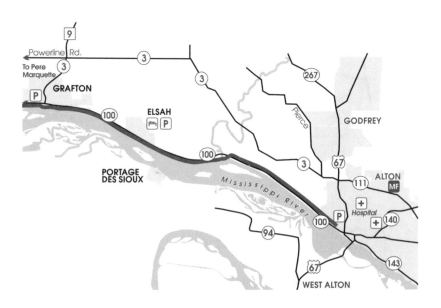

SYMBOL LEGEND

- Beach/Swimming
- Bicycle Repair
- Cabin
- Camping
- Canoe Launch
- First Aid
- Food
- Golf Course
- Information
- Lodging
- Multi-Facilities
- Parking
- Picnic
- Ranger Station
- Restrooms
- Shelter
- Trailhead
- Visitor Center
- Water
- Overlook/ Observation

TRAIL LEGEND

———————	Trail-Biking/Multi
·············	Hiking only Trail
••••••••••••	Hiking - Multi Use
▬▬▬▬▬	Snowmobiling only
= = = = = = =	Planned Trail
▬ ▬ ▬ ▬	Alternate Trail
———————	Road/Highway
+++++++++	Railroad Tracks

AREA LEGEND

	City, Town
	Parks, Preserves
	Waterway
	Marsh/Wetland
	Mileage Scale
★	Points of Interest
– –	County/State
♣	Forest/Woods

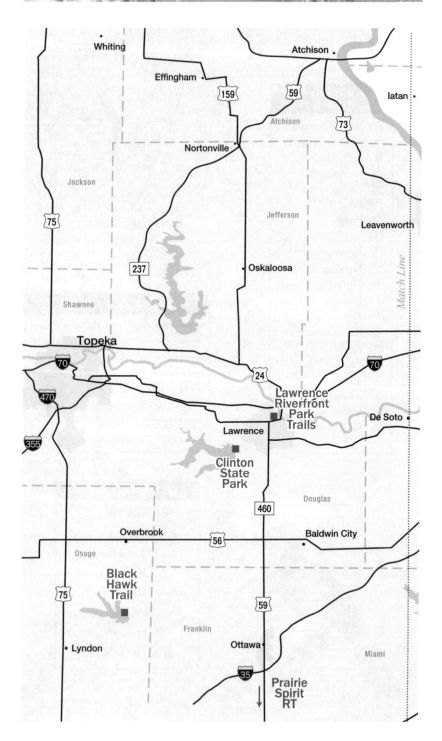

▲ Mountain Biking
■ Leisure Biking
◆ Both Leisure & Mountain Biking

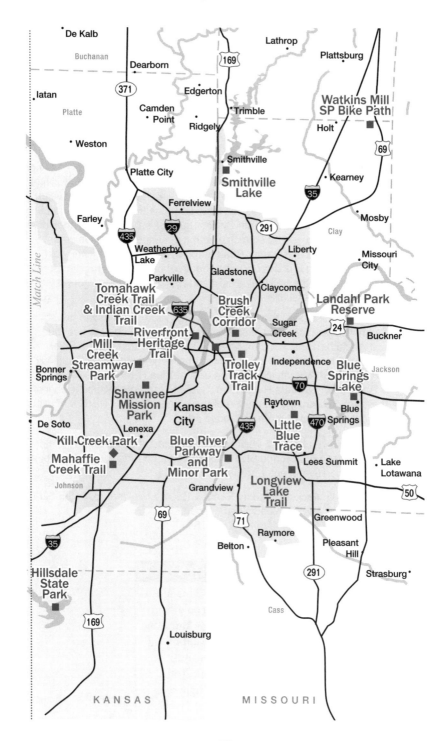

Blue River Parkway (Minor Park)

Trail Uses	🚲 🏃 🎧
Vicinity	Kansas City
Trail Length	12 miles
Surface	Natural, dirt
County	Jackson

Trail Notes   The Blue River Parkway, sometimes referred to as "Minor Park", is located along the Blue River in south Kansas City. Here you will find a scenic and quiet get-away. Within the parkway are several trails that wind along both sides of the Blue River. The trails begin near Red Bridge Road on the north and travels south of Martin City to 139th Street. There are additional trails, more frequently used by equestrians that continue west of Holmes Road to the Polo fields at Kenneth Road at the state line into Kansas. Just west of the road bed and a short distance south of the sign board, is a more challenging section of the trail that is tight and twisty as it winds through the woods and across several hills.

The trail on the west side of the river is an old roadbed, and easy to ride. For more of a challenge, there are several trail legs off the roadbed where the effort level would be considered moderate. On the east side of Blue River Road you'll find the effort level to be a more challenging moderate to difficult. The "Bo Ho Ca" and "Mountain" trails run east of Blue River Road and the "Wagon Trail" runs from Blue Ridge Blvd. South to the Power Substation just off 139th Street. Toward the south end of the Wagon Trail is "The Knob" with a 2-3 foot rock drop for the more advanced rider.

Getting There   Take I-435 west to Holmes Road, then south on Holmes Road for 3.5miles to Blue Ridge Blvd. Proceed east on Blue Ridge Blvd. for a quarter mile to the several entry points on your left.

Contact	Jackson County Parks & Recreation Dept. 816-795-8200
	22807 Wood Chapel Road
	Blue Springs, MO 64015

TRAIL LEGEND

————————	Trail-Biking/Multi
··············	Hiking only Trail
••••••••••••	Hiking - Multi Use
▬▬▬▬▬▬▬	Snowmobiling only
==========	Planned Trail
▬ ▬ ▬ ▬ ▬	Alternate Trail
————————	Road/Highway
+++++++++++	Railroad Tracks

Kansas City Metropolitan Area – Missouri

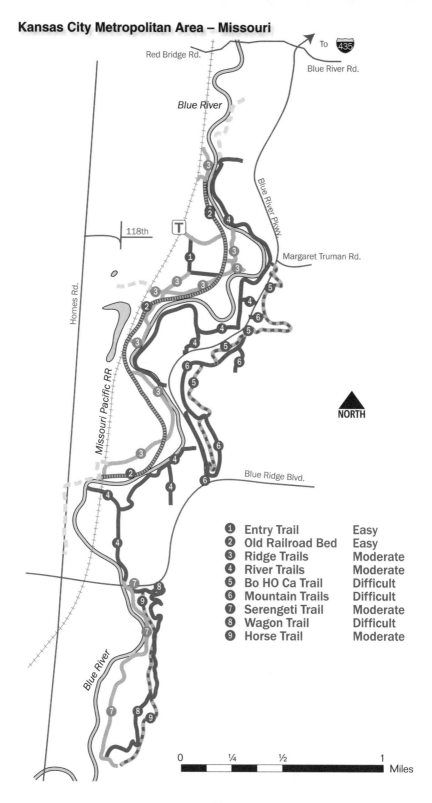

①	**Entry Trail**	**Easy**
②	**Old Railroad Bed**	**Easy**
③	**Ridge Trails**	**Moderate**
④	**River Trails**	**Moderate**
⑤	**Bo HO Ca Trail**	**Difficult**
⑥	**Mountain Trails**	**Difficult**
⑦	**Serengeti Trail**	**Moderate**
⑧	**Wagon Trail**	**Difficult**
⑨	**Horse Trail**	**Moderate**

Blue Springs Lake

Trail Uses

Vicinity — Blue Springs

Trail Length — 5 miles

Surface — Crushed gravel, roads

County — Jackson

Trail Notes Located in Blue Springs and Lee's Summit, this 720 acre lake provides many recreational facilities in addition to the hiking/biking trail, including camping, picnic shelters, a swimming beach, concessions and boat rentals. The surface of this 5 mile trail is crushed gravel, but because of spotty erosion, a mountain bike might be your better choice. The setting provides ample lake views with hills and beautiful vistas. The trail course becomes a loop by taking Liggett Road east or Chapel Road north from the parking area by the Park Administration Building.

Blue Springs Lake is a part of the U.S. Army Corps of Engineers Little Blue River Project for flood control and recreation development. It's located in Fleming Park, and is managed by Jackson County. Favored water sports include power boating, water skiing, tubing and jet skiing.

Getting There Blue Springs Lake is located in Jackson County's Flemming Park, about 9 miles from Kansas City. From I-470, exit East on Woods Chapel Road, Bowlin Road or Hwy 40 for park access.

Contact
Jackson County Parks   816-503-4802
22807 Woods Chapel Road
Blue Springs, MO 64105

Blue Springs Lake   816-795-1112
Woods Chapel Road
Blue Springs, MO 64105

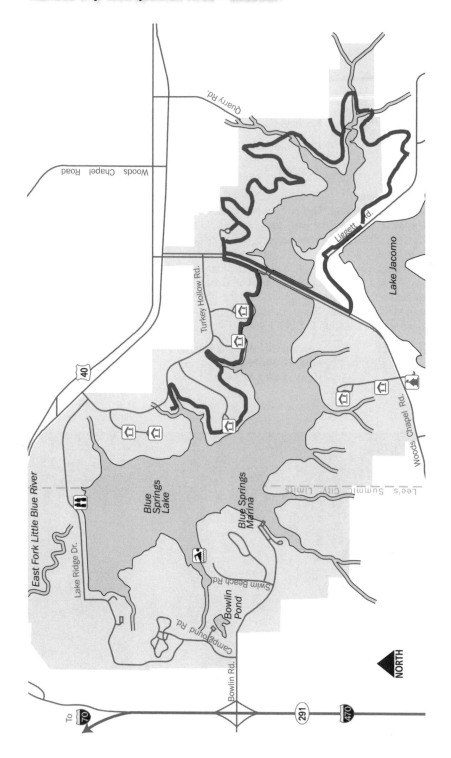

Brush Creek Corridor

Trail Uses	
Vicinity	Kansas City
Trail Length	5.5 miles
Surface	Concrete
County	Jackson

Trail Notes   The Brush Creek Corridor runs from the Blue River west to Belleview Street. The current trail extends from The Paseo to Roanoke Parkway. The corridor was designed to hold stormwater and provide an east-west pedestrian connection. The landscaped riverwalk is accented with lighting and fountains. It passes through the Country Club Plaza and provides access to the Nelson-Atkins Museum of Art, Volker Park, the Bruce R. Watkins Cultural Center and Brush Creek Park. Hours are from sunrise to sunset. There are plans to extend the greenway west to State Line Road and east to the Blue River. Brush Creek is a natural waterway that winds from Kansas into Missouri through Kansas City.

Contact
Kansas City Parks & Recreation Dept.   816-513-7500
4600 E. 63rd Street
Kansas City, MO 64130

Kansas City Metropolitan Area – Missouri

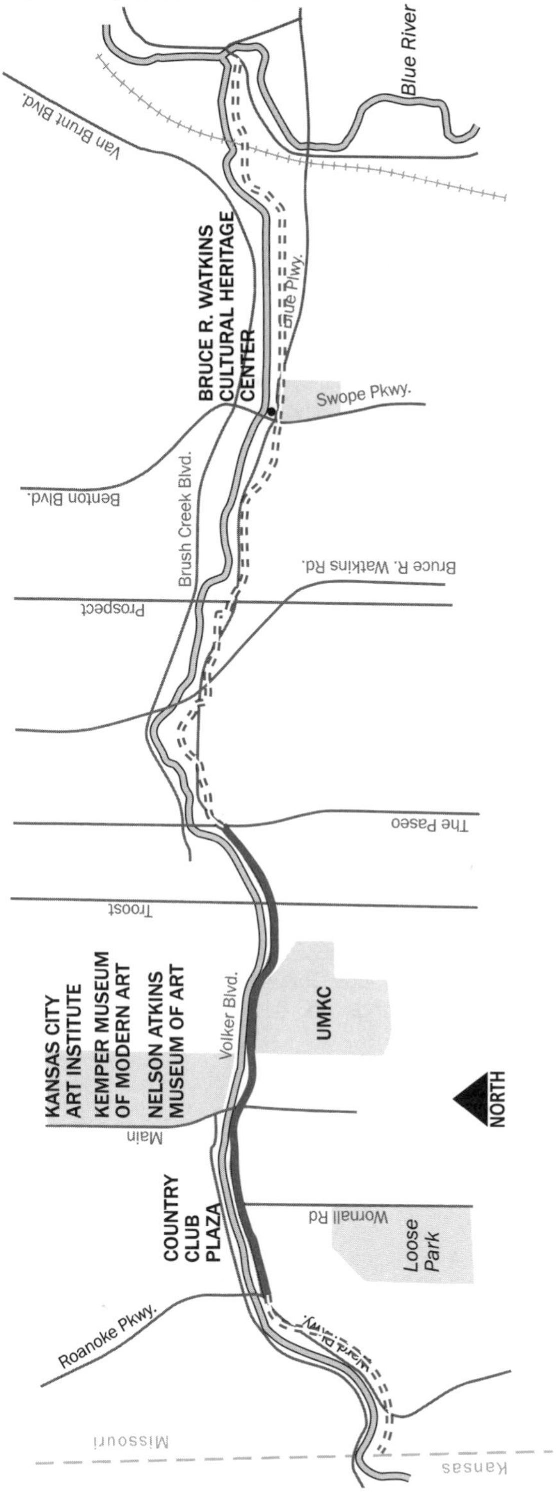

Landahl Mountain Bike Trail

Trail Uses	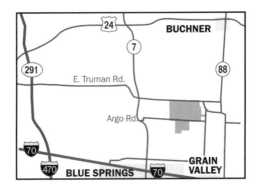
Vicinity	Blue Springs
Trail Length	9 miles
Surface	Natural, groomed
County	Jackson

Trail Notes   This 9 mile trail system consists of multiple loops, and is almost entirely tight single track. The trail course varies from extremely technical rocky stretches, with climbs on loose, rocky slopes, to long smooth descents. In the eastern section the grades are long, gradual and easy. As you head west, the grades become shorter, steeper, and more technical. The western section is steep and rocky. Beware of riding after a rain, as these trails can get very slick and muddy.

In season, drinking water is available at several areas in the park. Other park facilities include picnic areas, and camping. The setting is heavily wooded and quite scenic. These trails are maintained by Earth Rider Mountain Bike Club volunteers. The Club also developed the trail numbers and difficulty ratings for this trail system.

Getting There   From the intersection of I-70 and Hwy 7, by Blue Springs, take Hwy 7 north to Pink Hill Road. Turn east (right) and continue to Owens School Road, then turn north (left) and go to Argo Road. Turn east (right), going past the gun range on your left, up a hill to a gravel parking lot on your left. To get to the trail, go through the gate and follow the double-track into the woods to a signboard with a map of the trails.

Contact	Jackson County Parks & Recreation 22807 Woods Chapel Road Blue Springs, MO 64015	816-503-4890

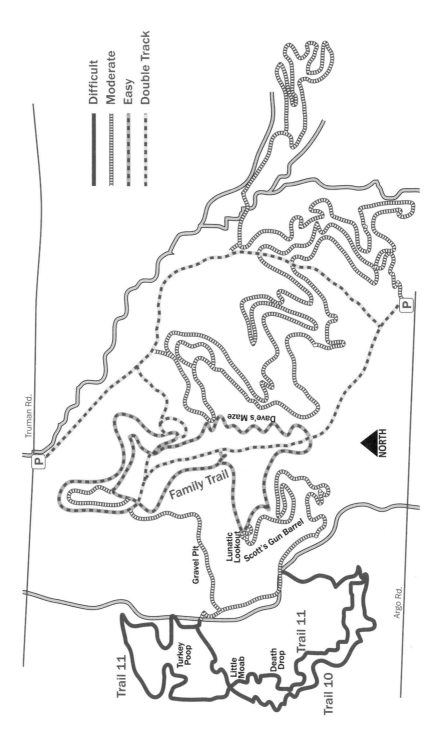

Little Blue Trace Trail

Trail Uses	🚲 🏃
Vicinity	Kansas City
Trail Length	11 miles
Surface	Limestone screenings
County	Jackson

Trail Notes   This multi-purpose trail is located in the center of Jackson County in eastern Independence along the Little Blue River. It runs from Blue Mills Road, north of Hwy 24, south to I-70. The trail is fairly level and is open from sunrise to sunset. Facilities along the trail include restrooms and picnic areas. The popular trailhead is east of Little Blue Parkway and north of I-70, across from the new strip mall.

Getting There   There are several access areas: Blue Mills road, Ripley Junction, Bunshu Road, MO Hwy 78 and R. D. Mize Road. There is also an access point planned in the Harman Heritage Center west of Little Blue Parkway. Ample parking is available at the shelter at Hwy 78, just west of Hwy 7, which is the north end of the trail. There is also limited parking near the south end of the trail on R. D. Mize Road.

Contact   Jackson County Parks and Recreation   816-795-8200
22807 Woods Chapel Road
Blue Springs, MO 64105

SYMBOL LEGEND

🏊	Beach/Swimming	MF	Multi-Facilities
🚲	Bicycle Repair	P	Parking
🏠	Cabin	🏓	Picnic
A	Camping	🧍	Ranger Station
🛶	Canoe Launch	🚻	Restrooms
+	First Aid	🏠	Shelter
🍴	Food	T	Trailhead
GC	Golf Course	🏛	Visitor Center
?	Information	💧	Water
🏨	Lodging	🔭	Overlook/ Observation

Kansas City Metropolitan Area – Missouri

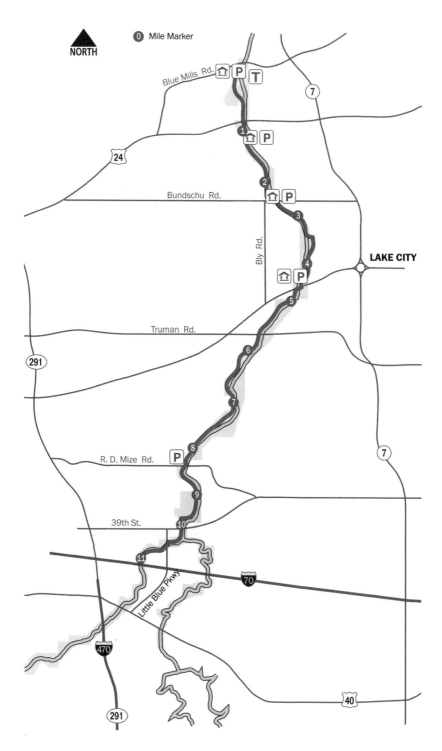

Longview Lake Trail

Trail Uses	🚲 🏃 ⛸
Vicinity	Kansas City
Trail Length	6 miles
Surface	Asphalt
County	Jackson

Trail Notes   The Longview Lake Trail runs along the western edge of Longview Lake from O'Donnell Park to Longview Shelter. The asphalt trail meanders through wooded areas and open prairie and connects the marina, swimming beach and several shelters. The 4,852 acre Landview Lake Park is open from sunrise to sunset, and includes a 930 acre lake area. Facilities include, a marina, campground, picnic areas and shelters, a beach, and camping.

Landview Lake Park is a part of the U.S. Army Corps of Engineers Little Blue River Project for flood control and recreation. It opened to the public in 1986. The park records over 1,000,000 visitors annually.

Getting There   Longview Lake Park is located south of Kansas City. From I-470, take Raytown Road (exit 4) south for 1 mile to the park entrance.

Contact   Jackson County Parks and Recreation   816-795-8200
2280-7 Woods Chapel Road
Blue Springs, MO 64105

US Army Corps of Engineers   816-761-6194
10698 E 109th Street
Kansas City, MO 64134

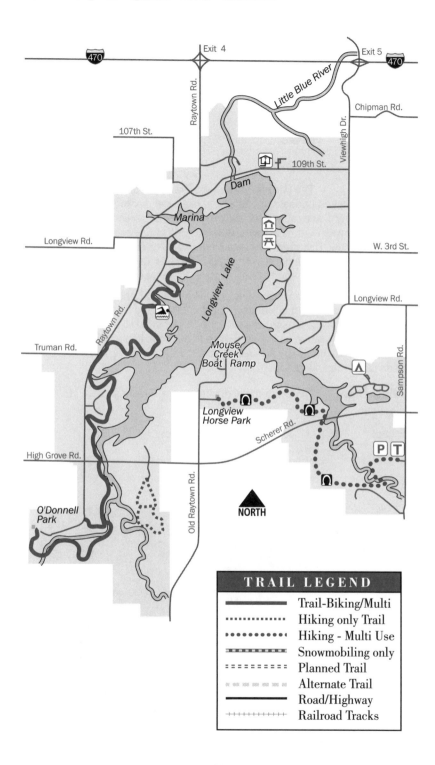

TRAIL LEGEND

——————	Trail-Biking/Multi
··············	Hiking only Trail
••••••••••	Hiking - Multi Use
▪=▪=▪=▪=▪	Snowmobiling only
= = = = = =	Planned Trail
▬ ▬ ▬ ▬ ▬	Alternate Trail
——————	Road/Highway
++++++++++	Railroad Tracks

Riverfront Heritage Trail

Trail Uses	🚲 🏃 ⛸
Vicinity	Kansas City
Trail Length	9 miles
Surface	Paved
County	Jackson

Trail Notes   The Riverfront Heritage Trails is a bi-state ribbon of green spaces, bicycle and pedestrian paths, and historical markers designed to link Kansas City's cultural and recreational history beginning at the riverfront where the city was born. The trail spans from SW Boulevard in Kansas City, MO to the Berkley Riverfront Heritage Park in the NE section. There is a short break in the trail under a train bridge. There is also a section of trail that crosses the Kansas/Missouri Stateline going to Kansas City.

The trail links the downtown business districts of both Kansas Cities, the Rivermarket and Richard L. Berkley Riverfront Park, the Central Industrial District, and the Westside, Quality Hill, and Strawberry Hill neighborhoods. It was designed to serve as an alternative to automobile transportation, and to provide scenic and to provide recreational amenities along the bi-state Kansas City urban riverfront.

Getting There   There are many access points. Trailheads are identified on the map.

Contact   Mid-America Regional Council
816-701-8387, 816-474-4240
A600 Broadway, Suite 300
Kansas City, MO 64105

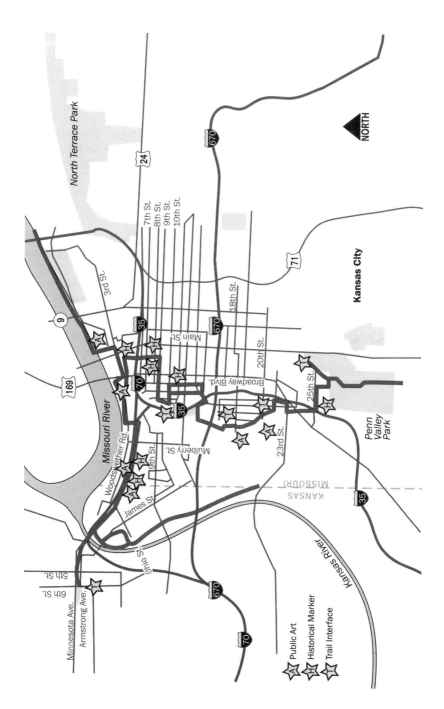

Smithville Lake (Crows Creek Trail)

Trail Uses	🚲 🚶 🐎
Vicinity	Smithville
Trail Length	16 miles
Surface	Natural
County	Clay

Trail Notes   This equestrian trail system follows the southern shores of Smithville Lake. The Shoreline Trail is identified with orange markers and is 10 miles long. The Boundary Trail is identified with white markers and is 6 miles long. They intersect, join and combine at several points, and are both double track and single track. The trail markers are green metal fence posts with orange or white paint tips. Some areas of the trails are clearly marked while others are hardly discernable. Effort level is moderate.

Smithville Lake was created in 1979 by damming the Platte River. The surface area of the lake is now over 7,000 acres, and is popular with boaters and fishermen. The setting is grassland prairie, gravel, woods, water crossings and gullies. Camping is available at Crows Creek Campground. Facilities include water, restrooms and showers. The trailheads are located at accesses 22, 23, 24, or from Crows Creek Park.

Getting There   From Smithville, take Hwy 159 north to CR W. Go east (right) for about 3 miles to the little community of Paradise. Turn right on Collins, and follow it across Smithville Lake past Camp Branch to the parking area.

Contact   Smithville Lake Visitors Center   816-532-0174
16311 Hwy DD North
Smithville, MO 64089

Clay County Dept. of Parks & Recreation
816-407-3400, 816-532-0803
17201 Paradesian
Smithville, MO 64089

Kansas City Metropolitan Area – Missouri

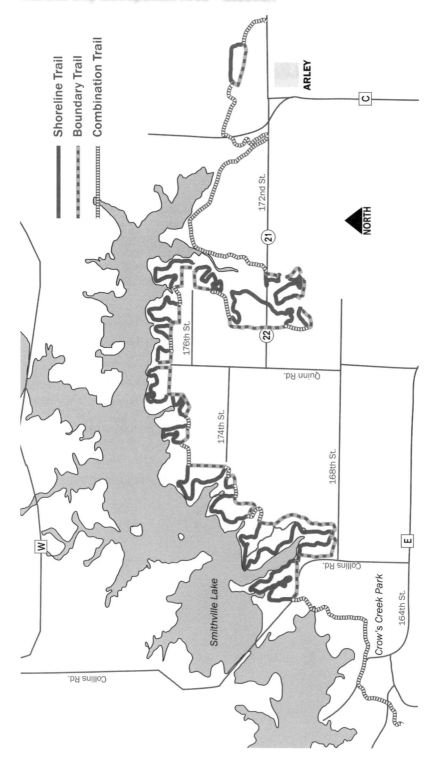

Trolley Track Trail

Trail Uses	🚲 🚶
Vicinity	Kansas City
Trail Length	6.5 miles
Surface	Limestone screenings, asphalt
County	Jackson

Trail Notes   The Trolley Track Trail is routed along a former trolley rail line, and was constructed in 1997. Currently it travels north/south between Volker Blvd. and Prospect Avenue. There are plans to extend it east to Prospect Avenue. Most of the trail is surfaced with crushed limestone, with some short sections of asphalt in areas that are subject to brief flooding. South of 85th Street the surface is asphalt. The trail is open from sunrise to sunset. There is public lighting from 59th Street to 62nd Terrace, and from Main to 85th Street.

Segments		
	Volker to 55th Street	0.8 miles
	55th to 62 Street	1.0 mile
	Meyer to 74th Street	1.5 miles
	75th Street to 85th Street	1.4 miles
	85th Street to Prospect	1.3 miles

Getting There   There are many access points. Parking is available at Brookside Park, the Wornall House Museum and at South Oak Park at 85th Street.

Contact	Kansas City Area Transportation Authority 816-356-0200
	1200 E. 18th Street
	Kansas City, MO 64108

Kansas City Metropolitan Area – Missouri

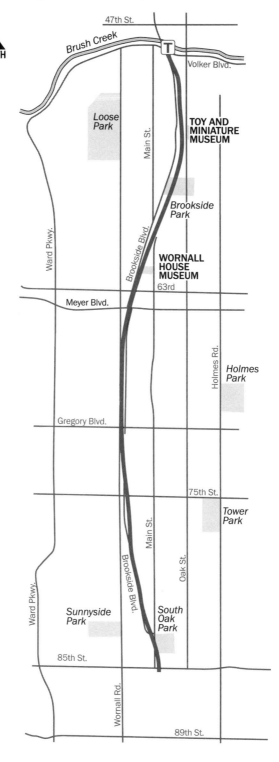

NORTH

47th St.

Brush Creek

Volker Blvd.

Loose Park

Main St.

TOY AND MINIATURE MUSEUM

Brookside Park

Brookside Blvd.

WORNALL HOUSE MUSEUM

63rd

Ward Pkwy.

Meyer Blvd.

Holmes Rd.

Holmes Park

Gregory Blvd.

75th St.

Tower Park

Main St.

Oak St.

Brookside Blvd.

Ward Pkwy.

Sunnyside Park

South Oak Park

85th St.

Wornall Rd.

89th St.

Watkins Mill State Park

Trail Uses   🚲 🏃 🐎

Vicinity   Kearney

Trail Length   3.8 miles

Surface   Asphalt

County   Clay

Trail Notes   The 3.8 mile asphalt bicycling and walking trail follows the shoreline of the William Creek Lake, and can be accessed at several points along the west side of the lake and from the northern picnic area. Bicycles are not permitted on the separate 3 mile long horse trail. There is a visitor center, picnic sites, swimming, tours and nearly 100 wooded campsites at the park.

The site was once the small community built by Waltus Watkins in the 1800's. Included in the 3,600 acres were an elegant home, three-story woolen mill, fruit-drying shed, smokehouse, brick kiln, sawmill, gristmill and acres of orchards and croplands. There is also a brick schoolhouse and church in the vicinity. Many of the original buildings have been restored, and tours are available.

Getting There   From Kansas City take Exit 8 north off I-70 onto I-435 northbound. Proceed on I-435 for 11 miles until it merges into northbound I-35. Continue north on I-35 for 15 miles, exiting at Kearney. Turn right onto eastbound Hwy 92 and continue east for 5 miles onto Route RA. Turn north (left) and go to the park entrance on the right.

From St. Joseph, take Hwy 36 east for 27 miles to Cameron. From there take I-35 south for 28 miles, exiting at Kearney. Turn left onto eastbound Hwy 92 and continue east for 5 miles to Route RA. Turn north (left) and go to the park entrance on the right.

Contact   Watkins Woolen Mill State Park   816-580-3387
26600 Park Road North
Lawson, MO 64602

Kansas City Metropolitan Area – Missouri

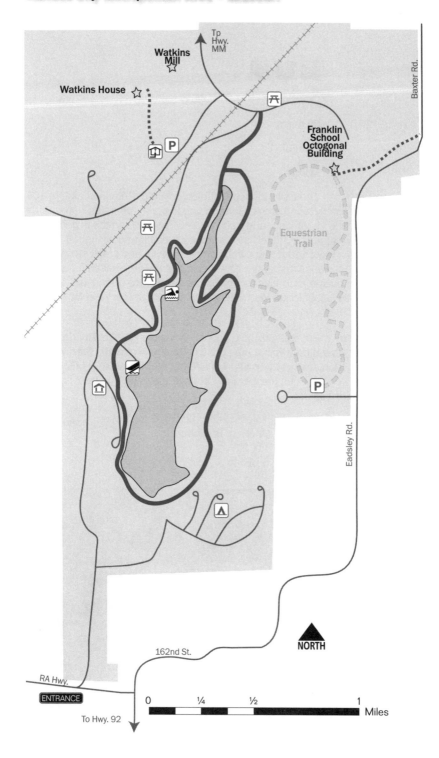

Watkins Mill

Tp Hwy. MM

Watkins House

Baxter Rd.

P

Franklin School Octogonal Building

Equestrian Trail

P

Eadsley Rd.

A

NORTH

162nd St.

RA Hwy.

ENTRANCE

To Hwy. 92

0   ¼   ½   1   Miles

Black Hawk Trail

Trail Uses	 (bike, hiking, horseback icons)
Vicinity	Overbrook
Trail Length	20 miles
Surface	Natural, dirt
County	Osage

Trail Notes   The trail runs along the shoreline of Pomona Lake, in 100 Mile Park. It is mostly single track. Surrounding the lake are mature groves of native trees and vegetation, and open prairie. The trail surface is generally loose dirt and rock, and is shared as a horseback riding and hiking trail. You will experience a few challenging climbs and descents, and creek crossings. Overall the effort level is moderate. The trail is often overgrown with weeds with patches of poison ivy. Insects can also be a nuisance during the summertime. It's a scenic trail with little traffic, and should be ideal for nature lovers.

Getting There   From Overbrook, take S. Shawnee Heights Road south for 7 miles to a gravel road with a sign pointing to 110 Mile Park. Turn west for 3 miles and then south, where you will see another sign to 100 Mile Park. The trailhead is on the right, just before you enter the park. The park is about 25 miles south of Topeka.

Contact	Pomona Project Office 913-453-2201
	US Army Corps of Engineers
	Route 1, Box 139
	Vassar, KS 66543

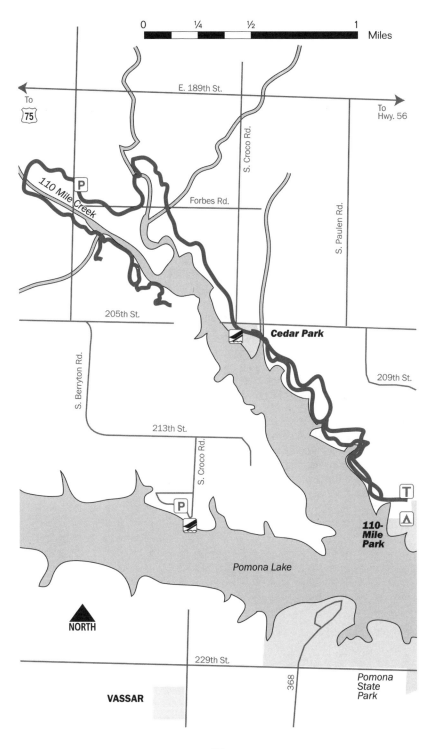

Pomona Lake

110-Mile Park

Cedar Park

Pomona State Park

VASSAR

NORTH

Clinton State Park

Trail Uses   🚲 🏃

Vicinity   Lawrence

Trail Length   15 miles

Surface   Natural

County   Douglas

Trail Notes   The Clinton Lake reservoir is one of the Corps of Engineers flood control projects in Kansas. Construction of the dam was started in 1972. There are two marked interconnecting, single-track trails that run along forested bluffs throughout the length of the park. These trails generally trace the wooded corridor between the lakeshore and the park roads, through the valleys and along the bays of the reservoir. There are short, steep climbs and descents, with tight turns, roots and rocks thrown in. Effort level is moderate to difficult and is certainly one of the better mountain biking locations in Kansas. The original trails were intended for hiking, but became open to mountain biking beginning in 1989. The Woodridge Park area on the west end of the lake is still limited to hikers and backpackers.

Facilities in the park include water, restrooms, picnic areas, camping, and swimming. The trails are sometimes not accessible following heavy rains. You might want to verify the park's gate hours. Between Monday & Thursday they are scheduled to be open from 4 pm to 8 pm, on Friday from 12 pm to 11 pm, on Saturday from 7 am to 11 pm, and on Sunday from 7 am to 9 pm.

Getting There   From Lawrence, take Hwy 40 west to CR 13. The state park entrance is a short distance to the north of the overlook and the Corps of Engineers Information Center. You can access the trail from the overlook area, from near the state park office on the road into the marina, or from parking area on a dirt road branching off the road into a maintenance area.

Contact   Clinton State Park   785-842-8562
           798 North 1415 Road
           Lawrence, KS 66049

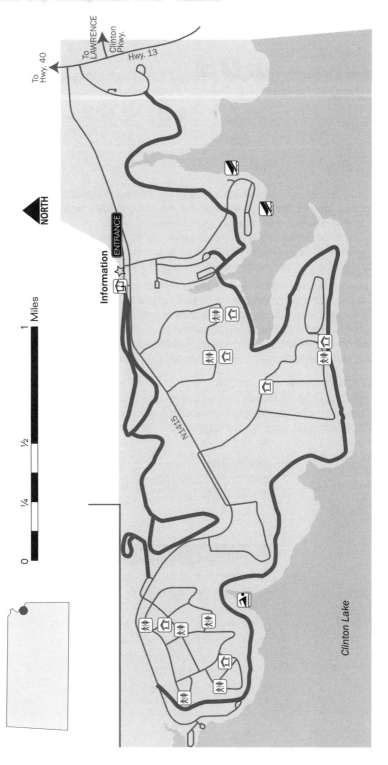

Hillsdale State Park

Trail Uses

Vicinity   Olathe

Trail Length   30 miles

Surface   Natural

County   Miami

Trail Notes   Hillsdale is one of the newest reservoirs in Kansas, completed in 1982 for flood control. It is located in the rolling hills of Miami County. There are 51 miles of shoreline and 4,500 acres of surface water. Vehicle day-use permits are required unless you park at the Corps of Engineer visitor center. Facilities include water, restrooms, a campground, and a beach. The nearby town of Hillsdale has a few small stores.

There are some 30 miles of marked and unmarked trails available to bicyclists and horseback riders. Most of the trail system is dirt single-track, but there is some grassy double-track alongside old roads and fence lines. Effort level varies all the way from easy to more difficult. You'll come across some steep climbs and descents, narrow brushy sections and rocks. The setting is mostly wooded with some open meadowland and limestone cliffs.

Getting There   From Olathe take Hwy 169 south, or from Paola take Hwy 169 to 255th Street, then west through Hillsdale for about 2 miles to the state park. You can park at the Corps of Engineers Visitor Center, the Marysville boat ramp 1.5 miles north of the visitor center or the windsurfing beach.

Contact   Hillsdale State Park   913-783-4507
                26001 West 255th Street
                Paola, KS 66071

TRAIL LEGEND	
————————	Trail-Biking/Multi
·············	Hiking only Trail
••••••••••••	Hiking - Multi Use
▪▪▪▪▪▪▪▪	Snowmobiling only
= = = = = = = = =	Planned Trail
▨ ▨ ▨ ▨ ▨ ▨	Alternate Trail
————————	Road/Highway
+++++++++++	Railroad Tracks

Kansas City Metropolitan Area – Kansas

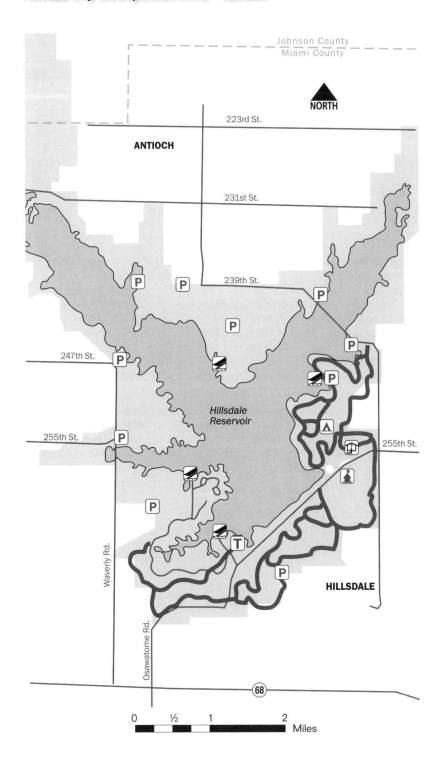

Indian Creek & Tomahawk Creek Trails

Trail Uses ⛰🚶🧗🏃

	Indian Creek	Tomahawk Creek
Vicinity	Overland Park	Overland Park
	Kansas City, Mo.	Leawood
Trail Length	24 miles	6 miles
Surface	Asphalt	Asphalt
Counties	Jackson, Johnson	Johnson

Trail Notes

Indian Creek Trail Greenway The Indian Creek Trail Greenway passes through Leawood, Overland Park, Olathe, and Kansas City, Missouri. It connects with Tomahawk Creek Trail, Pinehurst Park, Foxhill South Park, the Corporate Woods Business Park, Stroll Park, the Overland Park Golf Course and Water Works Park in Olathe. The Overland Park portion starts at the Foxhill South Park, at 109th and Elmonte, and follows the creek south and west to the Forest Creek Park at 125th and Pflumm. A connecting link continues south along Quivira towards the Tomahawk Creek Trail via 127th and Nieman. The trail expands westward toward Olathe's trail at Indian Creek and Pflumm.

The path is about 8 feet wide and there are mileage markers every half mile. The terrain is generally level and flat, although there are some steep grades for short distances. These include the route south of the creek between Nall and Lamar, near 105th and Conser, and along I-435, west of Antioch. The trail is open from sunrise to sunset.

Trailheads with parking lots:

> Foxhill South Park, 109th and Elmonte
> Foxhill North Park, Indian Creek Parkway and Roe
> Roe Park at 105th and Roe
> Indian Creek Recreation Center, 103rd and Marty
> Corporate Woods Founders' Park at 9711 W. 109th Street
> Indian Valley Park, 116th and Knox
> Quivira Park at 119th and Quivira

Tomahawk Creek Trail Greenway The trail runs through both Leawood and Overland Park. It connects Indian Creek Trail, Leawood Park, Tomahawk Park, Deer Creek Golf Course, Overland Park Community Park and St. Andrews golf Course. There are also plans to connect it to Black Bob Park and Heritage Park Golf Course. There is a bridle path located on some portions of the trail, and picnic facilities also located along the trail. The north trailhead is at Mission Road & I-435, and the south trailhead is at 127th Street west of Nall Road. Trail hours are sunrise to sunset.

Trailheads:

North terminus is at Mission Road & I-435

South terminus is at 127th Street west of Nall Road

Contacts   **Indian & Tomahawk Creek Trails**
City of Overland Park
Parks & Recreation   913-327-6630
6300 West 87th
Overland Park, KS 66212

City of Leawood Parks & Greenways   913-339-6700
4800 Town Center Drive
Leawood, KS 66211

Indian Creek Trail
City of Kansas City
MO Parks & Recreation   816-513-7500
4600 East 63rd Street
Kansas City, MO 64130

City of Olathe Parks Dept.   913-393-6038
200 West Sante Fe
Olathe, KS 66061

Indian Creek & Tomahawk Creek Trails (continued)

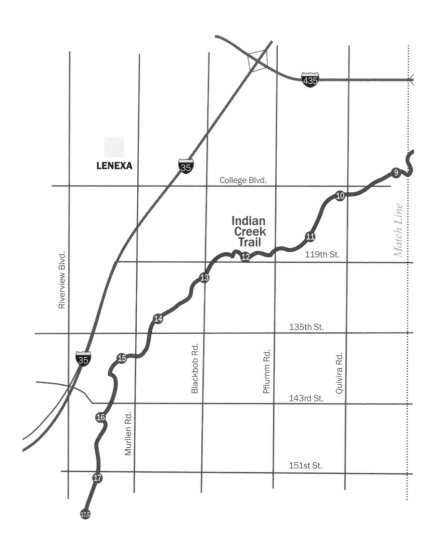

LENEXA

College Blvd.

Indian
Creek
Trail

119th St.

135th St.

143rd St.

151st St.

Riverview Blvd.

Murllen Rd.

Blackbob Rd.

Pflumm Rd.

Quivira Rd.

Match Line

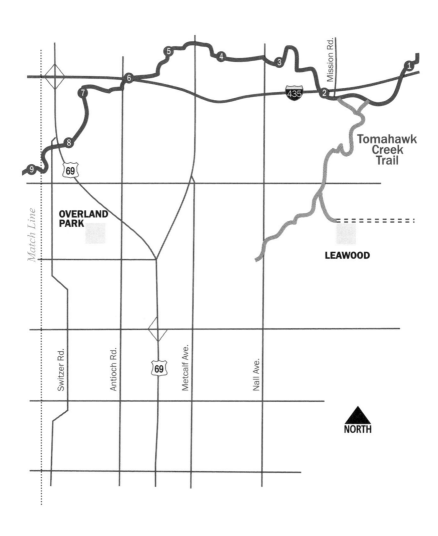

Tomahawk
Creek
Trail

OVERLAND
PARK

LEAWOOD

Match Line

Mission Rd.

Switzer Rd.

Antioch Rd.

Metcalf Ave.

Nall Ave.

69

435

69

NORTH

Kill Creek Trail

Trail Uses

Vicinity   Olathe, KS

Trail Length   3 miles   4.5 miles

Surface   Paved   Natural

County   Johnson

Trail Notes   There are approximately 3 miles of paved trail and 4.5 miles of mountain bike trail in 980 acre Kill Creek Park. Additional facilities include picnic shelters, a swimming beach and a marina with boat rentals. The setting is rolling landscape of low, forested hillside and valley floors of brush and natural grasses.

The 2.5 mile Eddy mountain bike trail is difficult. From the parking lot at shelter 1, take the paved path down the hill and away from the lake. At the bottom of the hill, turn right (north) along the creek, past the horseback trail intersection to the mountain bike trail entrance just east of the hiking trail. About a mile from the creek crossing is an intersection. Either direction will take you around the loop and back to the intersection. The 2 mile Hank trail has some rocky sections, with an effort level of easy to moderate. It can be reached by going past the Eddy entrance to the north end of the trail. Look for a brown sign.

Getting There   Kill Creek Park can be accessed at 33460 W. 95th Street in De Soto, or at Kill Creek Park near Creek Park near Shelter #1 on 11670 S. Homestead Lane in Olathe.

Contact   Kill Creek Park 913-831-3355
                  11670 Homestead Lane
                  Olathe, Kansas

TRAIL LEGEND	
————————	Trail-Biking/Multi
··············	Hiking only Trail
••••••••••	Hiking - Multi Use
▪▪▪▪▪▪▪▪	Snowmobiling only
==========	Planned Trail
▬ ▬ ▬ ▬ ▬ ▬	Alternate Trail
————————	Road/Highway
+++++++++++	Railroad Tracks

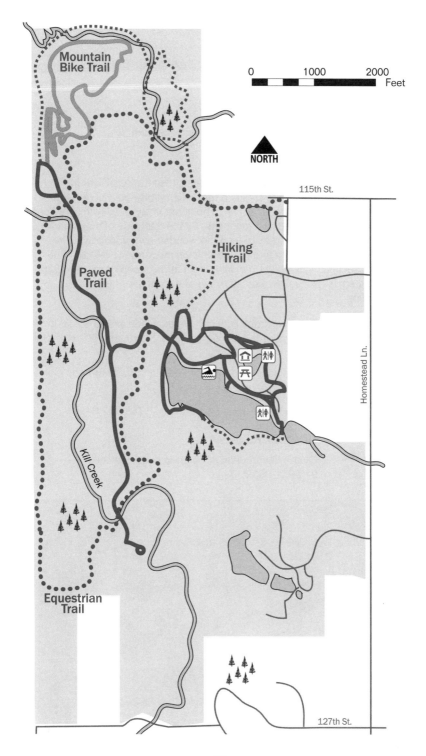

Lawrence Riverfront Park Trails

Trail Uses

Vicinity   Lawrence, KS

Trail Length   14 miles

Surface   Limestone screenings, packed earth

County   Douglas

Trail Notes   Located on the north side of the Kansas River in Lawrence, the Riverfront Park Trail is a recreational bike path on the top of the ten mile long levees along the river. The levee is surfaced with limestone screenings, and is easy and non-technical. By the east side of these paths are some 4 miles of single-track trail on the wooded river floodplain. The surface is mostly packed dirt and the effort level moderate to difficult. The challenging sections include short climbs, tight turns, steep drops, and logs. The trail system is accessible most of the year except after heavy rains, or spring thawing.

Getting There   The Riverfront Trail can be accessed at 2nd Street at the north end of the bridge, or near the junctions of US 24, 40, and 59 north of the I-70 interchange.

The floodplain trails can be accessed by going east on Elm to 8th and Oak Streets, near the boat ramp.

Contact   Lawrence Parks & Recreation   785-832-3450
                    PO Box 708
                    Lawrence, KS 66044

                    Olathe Community & Neighborhood Services
                    913-971-6659

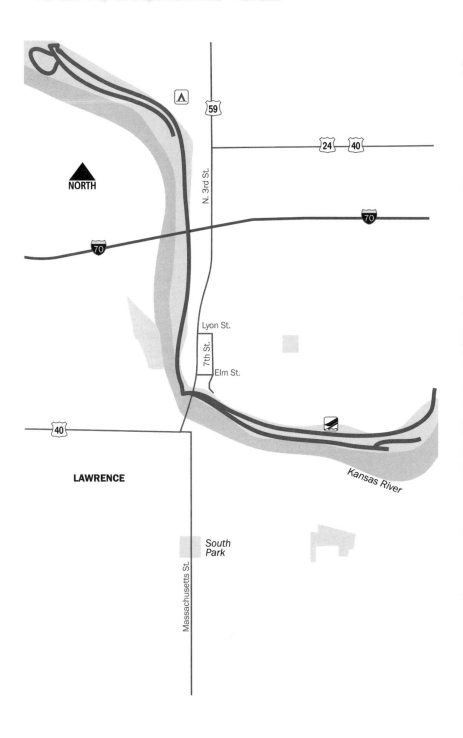

Mahaffie Creek Trail

Trail Uses

Vicinity   Olathe, KS

Trail Length   3.1 miles

Surface   Asphalt

County   Johnson

Trail Notes   The trail extends from Kansas City Road Park to the Mill Creek Streamway. There are multiple access points. The trail is 8 to 10 feet wide and is open during daylight hours. The setting is urban to woodland. The trails south of Harold Street are flat to gentle grade, while north of Harold to the Mill Creek Streamway, there are several steep grades with climbs and descents. The trail connector to Mahaffie Elementary School is a moderately steep grade from the primary trail to Nelson Road. When combined with the Mill Creek Streamway, there are approximately 18 miles of paved trail stretching north from Olathe to the Kansas River.

Getting There   There is access from Mahaffie Pond Park, at 1031 E. Cothrell Street, located near the Mahaffie Stagecoach Stop and Farm.

Contact   Olathe City Parks   913-971-8700
                   100 E. Santa Fe
                   Olathe, KS 66061

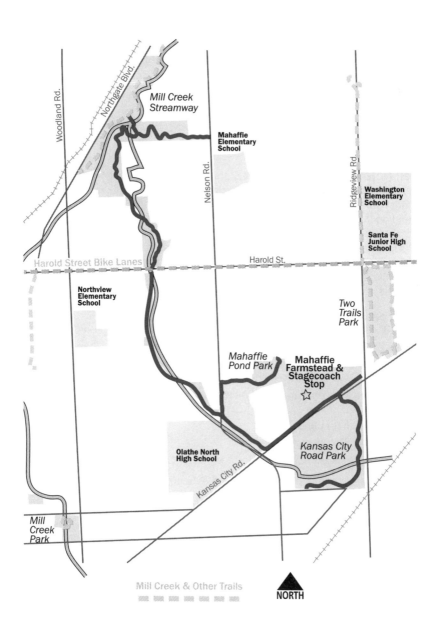

Mill Creek Streamway

Mahaffie Elementary School

Washington Elementary School

Santa Fe Junior High School

Harold Street Bike Lanes

Harold St.

Northview Elementary School

Two Trails Park

Mahaffie Pond Park

Mahaffie Farmstead & Stagecoach Stop

Olathe North High School

Kansas City Road Park

Kansas City Rd.

Mill Creek Park

Mill Creek & Other Trails

NORTH

Woodland Rd.

Northgate Blvd.

Nelson Rd.

Ridgeview Rd.

Mill Creek Streamway Park Trail

Trail Uses	ᗧ 🏃 👟 🐎
Vicinity	Olathe, KS
Trail Length	17 miles
Surface	Asphalt
County	Johnson

Trail Notes   The Mill Creek Streamway Park has over 17 miles of bicycle trails and four miles of horseback riding trails. The trail is one of the longest greenways in the Kansas City metropolitan area. It begins at Nelson Island on the Kansas River and heads south through Shawnee and Lenexa before reaching the southern end of Olathe. A ride on the trail will give you an opportunity to enjoy some streamside solitude, and to observe the local wildlife and forest lands featuring oaks, sycamores, and cottonwoods. There are picnic areas along the route, and a public phone at the Nelson Island terminus.

Access points with parking areas

4731 Wilder Road near the intersection with Holiday Drive in Shawnee

North of Shawnee Mission Parkway at 5946 Barker Road, Shawnee

19405 Midland Drive (west of I-435) at Shawnee Mission Parkway & Midland Drive in Shawnee

Shawnee Mission Park near Shelter 8 and north end of the dam in Lenexa

19865 W. 87th Lane, Lenexa

18460 W. 95th Street, Lenexa

11499 S. Millview, west of Ridgeview Road, Olathe

119th & Northgate, east of Woodland Avenue, Olathe

Contact	Johnson County Parks & Recreation	913-438-7275
	7900 Renner Road	
	Shawnee Mission, KS 66219	

Kansas City Metropolitan Area – Kansas

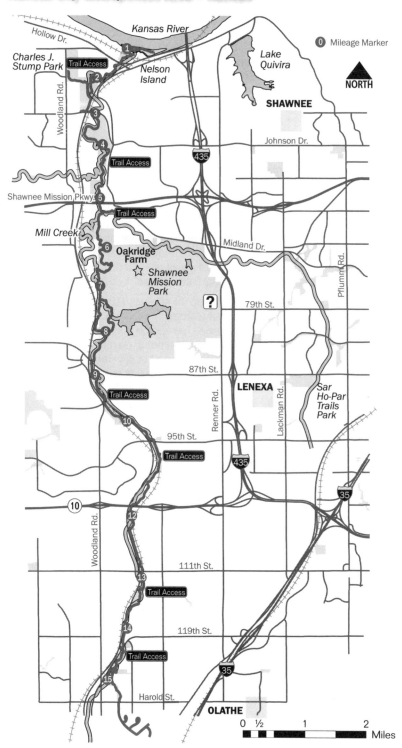

Prairie Spirit Rail Trail

Trail Uses	🚵 🏃 🛼
Vicinity	Garnett, Ottawa - KS
Trail Length	33 miles
Surface	Asphalt, crushed limestone
Counties	Franklin, Anderson

Trail Notes   The 33 mile trail is 12 foot wide and is surfaced with crushed limestone, except inside the city limits of Garnett and Ottawa where the surface is asphalt. It was built on old railway bed, and the grades are very moderate. The trail passes over several bridges overlooking ponds, creeks and the Marais Des Cygne River. Restrooms and picnic areas can be found in each community along the trail, and rest areas are placed strategically along the route. The trail within the city of Garnett also has decorative lighting.

There is a per-person trail permit required for persons 16 years and older to use the trail outside the city limits of Garnett and Ottawa. Within their city limits there is no charge. The daily permit fee can be purchased at self-pay stations located at the Ottawa, Princeton, Richmond, Garnett and Welda trailheads. Annual permits can also be purchased at several locations. The Prairie Spirit Trail is open during daylight hours outside the city limits of Garnett and Ottawa. While camping is prohibited along the trail corridor it is available at the North Lake Park in Garnett.

Upon completion of the next phase, the Prairie Spirit Rail Trail will span from Ottawa to Iola, for a total of more than 50 miles.

Getting There   The Prairie Spirit Rail Trail is just minutes away from Kansas City, Topeka, and Lawrence. The trail intersects I-35, US 59, US 169, US 68 and US 31.

Contact		
	Garnett Area Chamber of Commerce 419 S. Oak Garnett, KS 66032	785-448-6767
	Franklin County Tourism Bureau 2011 E Logan Ottawa, KS 66067	785-242-1411
	Franklin County Travel Bureau 2011 E. Logan Ottawa, KS 66067	785-242-1411

Kansas City Metropolitan Area – Kansas

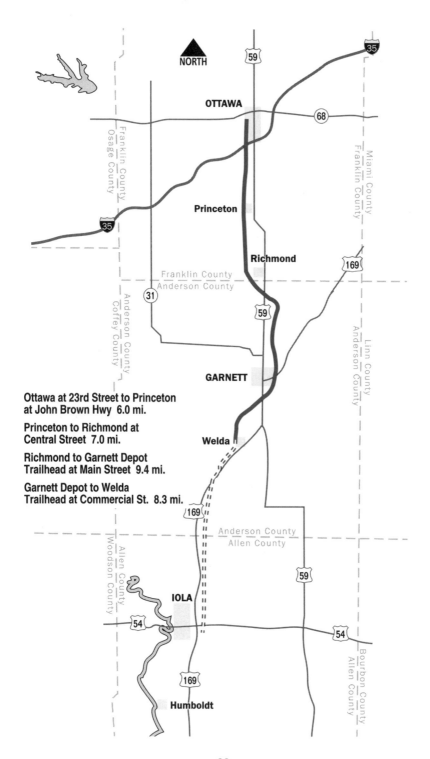

NORTH

OTTAWA

Princeton

Richmond

GARNETT

Welda

Ottawa at 23rd Street to Princeton
at John Brown Hwy 6.0 mi.

Princeton to Richmond at
Central Street 7.0 mi.

Richmond to Garnett Depot
Trailhead at Main Street 9.4 mi.

Garnett Depot to Welda
Trailhead at Commercial St. 8.3 mi.

IOLA

Humboldt

Franklin County / Osage County

Miami County / Franklin County

Franklin County / Anderson County

Anderson County / Coffey County

Linn County / Anderson County

Anderson County / Allen County

Allen County / Woodson County

Bourbon County / Allen County

Shawnee Mission Park

Trail Uses

Vicinity	Lenexa, KS
Trail Length	5 miles
Surface	Natural
County	Johnson

Trail Notes   The 1,250 acre Shawnee Mission Park is the largest in Johnson County. The mountain biking trail is located on the north side of the 150 acre Shawnee Mission Lake. The series of loops making up the trail are mostly single-track with a moderate effort level. Although the dirt track is generally smooth, there are sections of logs, low branches, sharp corners and rocks. The trail can be accessed by way of a park road that circles the lake. There is also a connector to the 11 mile asphalt paved Mill Creek Streamway Trail just to the west of the park.

Facilities at the park include water, restrooms, picnic areas, shelters, boating, concessions, tennis courts, and a swimming beach. There are separate nature and horseback riding trails. The Barley Visitor Center is located at the park entrance. This is also the headquarters for the Johnson County Parks and Recreation District. The general setting, in addition to the lake, consists of marshes, forests, meadows and ponds.

Getting There   From I-435, take Exit 3/87th Street west, then north (right) onto Renner Road. The park entrance is one mile further. From the entrance take Barkley Drive through the park to the trailhead parking lot at the end of the dam. The paved Mill Creek Streamway bike trail can also be reached from this trailhead.

Contact

Shawnee Mission Park   913-888-4713
7900 Renner Road
Shawnee, KS 66219

Johnson County Parks & Recreation   913-438-7275

AREA LEGEND	
	City, Town
	Parks, Preserves
	Waterway
	Marsh/Wetland
	Mileage Scale
★	Points of Interest
– –	County/State
	Forest/Woods

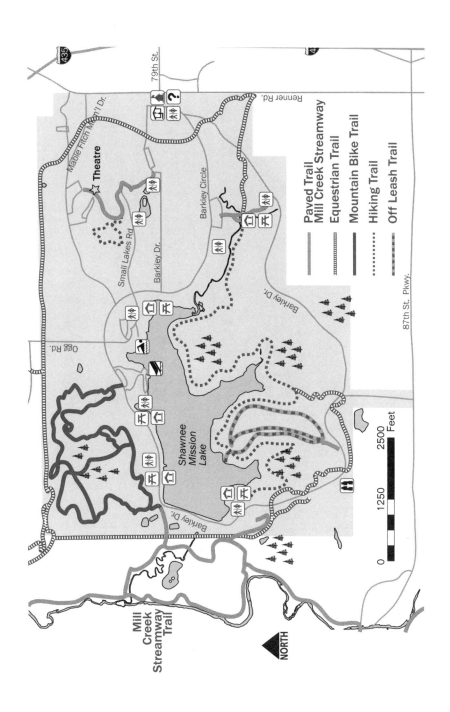

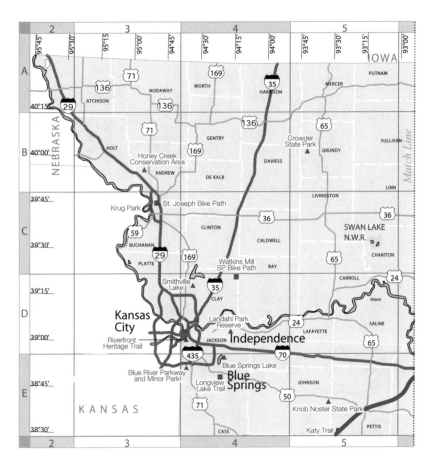

Binder Trail

Trail Uses	🚴 🚶
Vicinity	Jefferson City
Trail Length	12.7 miles
Surface	Natural, groomed
County	Cole

Trail Notes   Binder Park, with 644 acres, is Jefferson's City largest park. It's located off Rainbow Drive and Henwick Lane west of Jefferson City. In addition to a beautiful 150 acre lake, Binder Park provides numerous picnic sites, a picnic shelter, a RV campground with laundry and showers, a good ramp, and a playground. Canadian Geese and Blue Herons can frequently be seen at the lake during the migration season.

Fred. C. Binder established a trust fund in 1918 to build a park as a memorial to his father, himself, and his son. The property was purchased from the owners in 1965-6, and the Department of Conservation then began construction of the 155 acre fishing lake.

Inset

Green Loop	NW	3.5 miles
Blue Loop	W	3.9 miles
Red Loop	SW	1.7 miles
Loop	E	3.6 miles

Getting There   The entrance to Binder Park is off Hwy. 50 West, approximately 2 miles past Capital Mall.

Contact   Jefferson City Parks, Recreation & Forestry
573-634-6527, 573-634-6482

TRAIL LEGEND	
▬▬▬▬▬▬	Trail-Biking/Multi
··············	Hiking only Trail
●●●●●●●●●●	Hiking - Multi Use
▬▬▬▬▬▬	Snowmobiling only
==========	Planned Trail
▬ ▬ ▬ ▬ ▬	Alternate Trail
▬▬▬▬▬▬	Road/Highway
+++++++++	Railroad Tracks

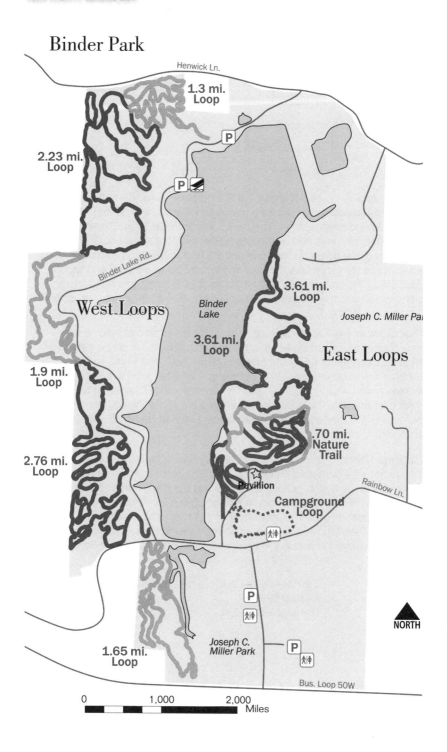

Binder Park

Henwick Ln.

1.3 mi. Loop

P

2.23 mi. Loop

P

Binder Lake Rd.

West Loops

Binder Lake

3.61 mi. Loop

Joseph C. Miller Pa

3.61 mi. Loop

East Loops

1.9 mi. Loop

2.76 mi. Loop

.70 mi. Nature Trail

Pavilion

Campground Loop

Rainbow Ln.

P

P

Joseph C. Miller Park

Bus. Loop 50W

NORTH

1.65 mi. Loop

0   1,000   2,000
                          Miles

Crowder State Park

Trail Uses   🚲 🚶 🎧

Vicinity   Trenton

Trail Length   15 miles

Surface   Natural, groomed

County   Grundy

Trail Notes   Much of this 1,912 acre park is covered with thick forest with a diverse population of trees, plants and flowers. It is noted for its rolling green hills and deep ravines. The park is named after Major General Enoch H. Crowder, who was nurtured in the hills of northern Missouri. One of the highlights of the ride is the junction of the Thompson and Weldon Rivers where there is a large beach beckoning you for some sunning and wading. Facilities at the park include a camping area, with restrooms and showers, picnic areas and the 18 acre Crowder Lake in the center of the park, open to boating and fishing.

The 3.2 miles Tall Oaks Trail loop is probably the most challenging with rock outcroppings and some tight, twisty turns. The trail is single-track, with an .8 mile connector on an old roadbed. The Thompson River Trail is a combination of double-track and old roads. The effort level is easy although there is a challenging climb. The two-loops making up this trail provides some great scenery. The River Forks Trail is fairly easy if ridden counterclockwise because of the grades you will experience. The Red Bud Trail is limited to hiking only

Getting There   From Trenton take Hwy 6 west for 3 miles to Hwy 146, then right to the park road (Hwy 128). Proceed north on Hwy 128 for a mile to the swimming beach parking lot. You'll find the River Forks Trail at the north end of the lot, or cross the dam to get to the Tall Oaks Trail. To get to the Thompson River Trail from Hwy 146 at Hwy. 128, continue on Hwy. 146 for another 1.3 miles west to Edinburg. Take 52nd Avenue NW north for 2.5 miles to Dove Lane at a T intersection. Take a right for 1/3 mile to the trailhead.

Contact   Crowder State Park   660-359-6473
                76 Hwy 128
                Trenton, MO 64683

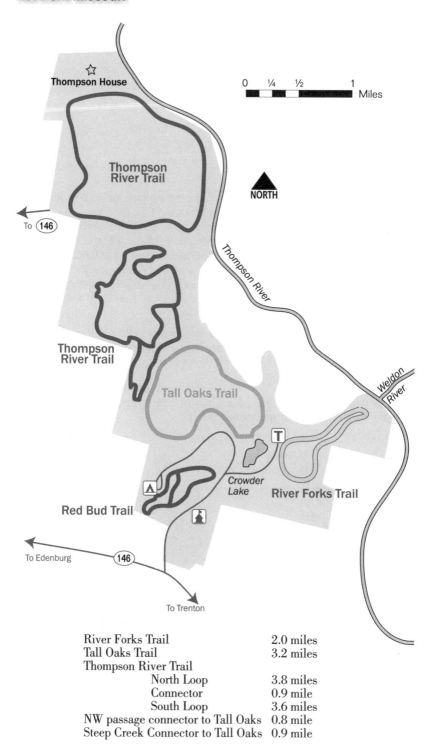

Thompson House

Thompson River Trail

To 146

NORTH

0 ¼ ½ 1 Miles

Thompson River

Thompson River Trail

Weldon River

Tall Oaks Trail

Crowder Lake

River Forks Trail

Red Bud Trail

To Edenburg 146

To Trenton

River Forks Trail		2.0 miles
Tall Oaks Trail		3.2 miles
Thompson River Trail		
	North Loop	3.8 miles
	Connector	0.9 mile
	South Loop	3.6 miles
NW passage connector to Tall Oaks		0.8 mile
Steep Creek Connector to Tall Oaks		0.9 mile

Graham Cave State Park

Trail Uses	🚶
Vicinity	Montgomery City
Trail Length	3 miles
Surface	Natural
County	Montgomery

Trail Notes   While currently limited to hiking only, be sure to visit the cave and the park museum if you can take the time from your trail riding. Graham Cave was the first archaeological site in the United State to be designated a National Historic Landmark in 1961. Artifacts have been uncovered revealing human use date back as early as 10,000 years ago. Clues to the lifestyle of the ancient Dalton and Archaic period Native American were discovered. The park features an unusual sandstone cave that once sheltered long ago human occupancy. The cave is 16 feet tall, 120 feet wide and 100 feet deep.

Several trails wind throughout the park's forests and glades. There is access to boating on the Loutre River. Picnic shelters and a wooded camping area is available.

Getting There   Take I-70 to MO TT, then west on MO TT for 2 miles to the park entrance. There is trail access from the parking lot near the cave, or from the upper picnic area and campground.

Contact	Graham Cave State Park	573-564-3476
	217 Hwy TT	
	Montgomery City, MO 63361	

Graham Cave   Photo courtesy of the Missouri Department of Natural Resources

Northern Missouri

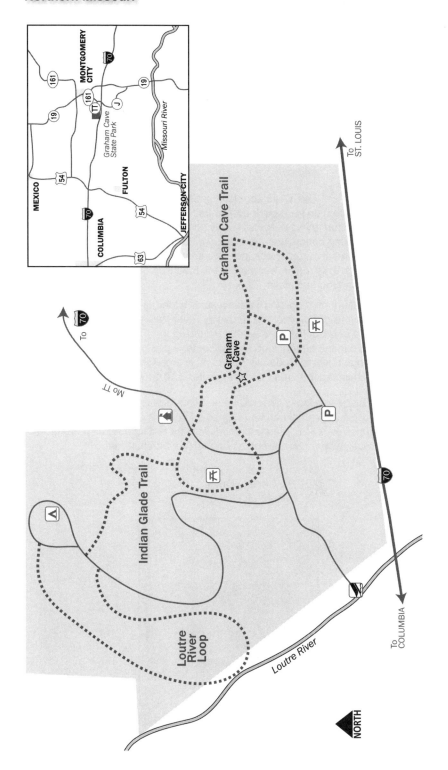

Honey Creek Conservation Area

Trail Uses	🚵 🚶 ⛺
Vicinity	Savannah
Trail Length	13 miles
Surface	Hard pack & gravel roads
County	Andrew

Trail Notes   The 1,148 acre Honey Creek Conservation Area is a 13 mile trail system on hard pack double-track roads and short gravel road sections. The effort level is easy with only some short, steep grades. The trails pass through bottomland fields and forested hillsides. Farming and haying complement current habitat development, such as tree, shrub and grass plantings. This region was part of the Platt Purchase between the U.S. government and the Indians in 1836.

On the 5.5 mile north loop, you'll pass a small waterfall on Honey Creek and then climb to a terrific view of the Nodaway River Valley. The 7.5 mile south loop follows a creek in the hollow before climbing to open ridge-top fields. You may want to ride the bottom loop clockwise, for if you ride counterclockwise there is a slope down to Nodaway River that is probably too steep for most to climb. The conservation area offers campsites, but no water.

Getting There   Honey Creek Conservation Area is located 15 miles northwest of St. Joseph. It can be reached by taking the Hwy 59 exit at Fillmore. Cross over I-29 Interstate and follow the blacktop road south until it turns to gravel, where you will find a parking area on your right.

Contact	Missouri Dept. of Conservation 816-271-3100
	701 NE College Drive
	St. Joseph, MO 64507

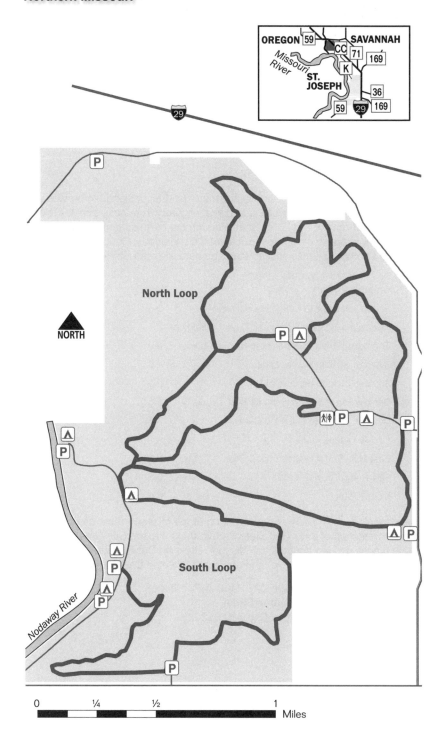

Jefferson City Greenways

Trail Uses	
Vicinity	Jefferson City
Trail Length	8 miles
Surface	Paved, crushed stone
Counties	Cole, Callaway

Trail Notes   This greenway is a multi-use trail designed to provide a safe alternative for biking, walking and skating away from busy streets. The trail extends from the Katy Trail State Park on the north side of the Missouri River to the intersection of West Edgewood Drive and S. Country Club Drive. There is another half mile section starting near Lafayette Street & Stadium Blvd.

Greenway Trail	Miles
Edgewood Drive to Shermans Hollow	0.5
Fairground Road to Edgewood Drive Parking Lot	2.1
Edgewood Drive Parking Lot to Stadium Blvd.	0.9
Stadium Blvd. to Wicker Lane	1.0
Stadium Blvd. to Satinwood Drive	0.5
Dunklin Street Trailhead to MO DOT District 5	1.0
Duensing Ballfield to Linden Drive	0.4
Park & Fitness Trails	
East Mille Street Neighborhood Park	0.3
Ellis-Porter/Riverside Park	0.3
McKay Park	0.6

Parking   There is parking north of the Missouri River on Katy Road at the connection of Katy Trail State Park to the Jefferson City Greenway. There also is parking south of the Missouri River on Dunklin Street, Kansas Street, West Edgewood Drive, and on Fourth Street in Cedar City.

Contact   Jefferson City Parks & Recreation   573-634-6482
427 Monroe Street
Jefferson City, MO 65202

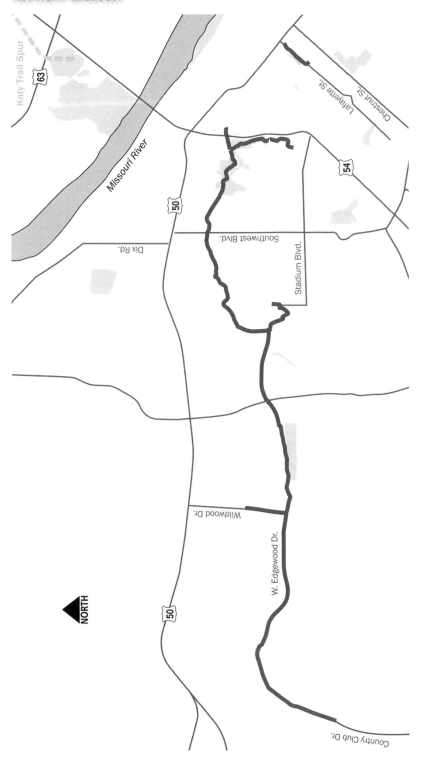

Katy Trail State Park

Trail Uses   🚲 🏃

Vicinity   St. Charles, Jefferson City, Clinton

Trail Length   225 miles

Surface   Crushed stone

Counties   St. Charles, Warren, Montgomery, Callaway, Boone, Cooper, Howard, Pettis, Henry

Trail Notes   Katy Trail State Park is built on the former Missouri-Kansas-Texas (MKT) Railroad corridor. It ceased operations from Machens in St. Charles County to Sedalia in Pettis County in 1986. The majority of the trail follows the Missouri River. You will frequently find yourself between the river on one side and towering bluffs on the other as you travel along the trail. The ride takes you through many types of landscapes, including pastureland, rolling farm field, dense forests, wetlands, remnant prairies and deep valleys. Spring and fall are the most popular seasons for extended rides. Spring brings out the flowering dogwood and redbud, while the fall shows off the rich reds and oranges of sugar maple, sumac and bittersweet. Summers can be hot and humid.

The 225 mile Katy Trail is the longest rail-to-trail conversion in the country, running from St. Charles west to Clinton. There are mile markers throughout its length. The entire trail is open to bicyclists and hikers, but horseback riding is allowed only between Calhoun and the Sedalia Fairgrounds trails, a total distance of approximately 25 miles. The surface is hard packed crushed stone. The trail is very flat, rarely exceeding a 2 % grade. Bike rentals are available at several trailside bike shops. Efforts are underway to extend the trail to Kansas City.

For a very detailed description of the trail and the many sight seeing opportunities along its route, refer to the book titled 'The Complete Katy Trail Guidebook' by Brett Dufur.

Contact   Missouri Dept. of Natural Resources   800-334-6946
320 First Street
Boonville, MO 65233

Shuttle Services

Active Trips	660-826-1188	
B & L Shuttle	660-221-4406	Sedalia, MO
Creasons Katy Trail Shuttle Services	573-694-2027	McKittrick, MO
Katy Trail Shuttle Service	636-497-5812	St. Charles, MO
Rendleman Home B & B	573-236-4575	Bluffton, MO
Bed & Breakfast & camping available		
T. C. Tours	314-739-5180	Bridgeton, MO
Also a Tour Organizer		
Trailrider Sports	877-875-2453	Clinton, MO
Bike repair rental available		

Directions

From the East   Where you should park your car for trail access really depends on what section of the trail you choose to ride. If you're looking to ride along river bluffs, head out past Rhineland. If it's wooded areas and some suburbia, the St. Charles or other eastern parking areas will do. For the easiest and quickest way to get to the Katy Trail from east of the Missouri River here are some suggestions:

Six miles from the 270/Page intersection is the Page Avenue/364 Bridge with a parking lot. From the parking lot is a mile ramp down to the trail, which is only 3 miles from the end of the trail in St. Charles.

There is parking at Creve Coeur Park with a 3.6 mile connector to the Katy Trail. The connector also provides some scenic views as you cross over the Missouri River.

The popular St. Charles Trailhead parking area can accommodate up to 200 cars and is right next to the Lewis & Clark Boathouse parking lot.

The Greens Bottom trailhead is at mile 45.7, and some six miles from the eastern end of the trail. From Hwy 40 the trailhead is 18 miles from the Chesterfield Mall, or12 miles on Page/364 from the Page/270 intersection.

The Weldon Spring Trailhead is at mile 56 and 16 miles from the end of the trail, but be aware that the turnoff from Hwy 94 is not very well marked.

Taking Hwy 94 south, you'll come to trailheads and parking in Defiance, at mile 59; Matson, at mile 60.6; Augusta, at mile 66; and Dutzow, at mile 74

From the West   Clinton or Sedalia gets you to the western section of the trail with its surrounding farmland, while Boonville or Rocheport brings you to the Missouri River.

Clinton is the western end of the trail and about 75 miles from Kansas City, while Sedalia is some 90 miles from Kansas City.

To get to the trail at the Missouri River, you'll have to go about 100 miles east from Kansas City where you will bike across it. The trail links up again with the river at Rocheport another 13 miles east. Just west of Rocheport you'll go through the famous Rocheport tunnel, and southeast, you'll have the river along side.

Bed & Breakfast

There are over 75 Bed and Breakfast Inns that can be found on or near the Katy Trail. Too many to list in this book, but a complete list can be found by going to the web at www.bikekatytrail.com or contact:

Bed & Breakfast Inns of Missouri
204 E. High St.
Jefferson City, MO 65101

Phone: 800-213-5642 Email: info@bbim.org

Katy Trail State Park (continued)

Camping

Camping is not allowed along the trail itself, but the following is a listing sequenced by distance from the mile markers:

Location	Camp/Distance from Trail	Mile Marker	Phone
St. Charles	Sundermeier RV Park 111 Transit	39	636-940-0111
Augusta	Klondike Park	64.1	636-949-7535
Dutzow	Dutzow Deli & Restaurant 11861 E. Hwy 94	74	
Marthasville	Scenic Cycles 292 Boone Monument Rd	75.9	636-433-2909
Marthasville	Community Club Park 601 One St.	78	636-433-2822
Marthasville	Choo Choos Frozen Custard & Camping 600 Depot St.	78.1	636-433-2488
Bluffton	Steamboat Junction Campground 199 Hwy 94	110.7	314-831-4807
Bluffton	Rendleman Home B& B 173 Hwy 94	111	573-236-4575
Portland	River's Edge RV Park & Campground 10512 Main Cross Street	115.9	573-676-3540
Steedman	S.O.B.'s	121.4	573-676-3220
Hartsburg	American Legion Park	153.6	573-636-9585
Hartsburg	Busch's Landing	153.6	573-657-2609
Hartsburg	Hartsburg Inn 25 South First Street	153.6	573-657-0071
Wilton	Riverview Traders 18300 River Rd.	157.4	573-657-1095
Easley	Cooper's Landing	162.5	573-657-2544
Huntsdale	Katfish Katy's	171.7	573-447-3939
Rocheport	Davisdale Conservation Area	182.1	573-884-6861
New Franklin	Katy Roundhouse 50 feet 1893 Katy Drive	188	660-848-2232
Boonville	Bobber Restaurant & Campground I-70 at Hwy B	191.8	660-882-7135
Sedalia	Countryside RV & Campground Hwy 65 S	229	660-827-6513
Sedalia	Missouri State Fairgrounds 0.6 mile Hwy 65 & 16th St.	229	660-530-5600
Windsor	Farrington Park 0.9 mile	248	660-647-5804
Clinton	Lester Foster Music Park 5 miles (during bluegrass festivals)	264.6	660-885-6457

Wineries

The Katy Trail cuts through Missouri's Wine Country, with numerous wineries near the trail. You can combine your Katy Trail with a little wine tasting, sampling some fine winds along the way.

St. Charles	Winery of the Little Hills 501 S. Main	636-946-9339
Matson	Sugar Creek Winery125 Boone Country Ln.	636-987-2400
Augusta	Augusta Winery5601 High St. at Jackson	636-228-4301
	Balducci Vineyards 6601 Hwy 94 South	636-482-8466
	Montelle Winery Highway 94 S.	636-228-4464
	Mount Pleasant Winery	800-467-WINE
Dutzow	Blumenhof Vineyards PO Box 30	800-419-2245
Hermann	Hermann Hill Vineyard & Inn711 Wein St.	573-486-4456
	(2.75 miles from the trail)	
Rocheport	Les Bourgeois Winery & Bistro	800-690-1830
	12800 Hwy BB at I-70	

Riding the Katy Trail   *Photo courtesy of Trailnet, Inc.*

Katy Trail State Park (continued)

Northern Missouri

All photos courtesy of Trailnet, Inc.

Photo courtesy of the Missouri Department of Natural Resources

Trailhead Distances & Facilities

Trailhead	From	To	Miles	Marker	Facilities		
St. Charles	0	225.1	0	39.5	P	👫	
Greens Bottom	6.2	218.9	6.1	45.7	P	👫	
Weldon Spring	16.5	208.6	10.3	56.0	P	👫	
Defiance	19.5	205.6	3.0	59.0	P		
Matson	21.2	203.9	1.6	60.6	P	👫	
Augusta	26.8	198.3	4.7	66.3	P	👫	
Dutzow	34.5	190.6	7.7	74.0	P	👫	
Marthasville	88.2	186.9	3.7	77.7	P	👫	
Treloar	44.9	180.2	6.7	84.4	P	👫	
McKittrick	61.3	163.8	16.4	100.8	P	👫	
Portland	76.4	148.7	15.1	115.9	P		
Mokane	85.5	139.6	9.1	125.0	P	👫	
Tebbetts	91.7	133.4	6.2	131.2	P	👫	
North Jefferson	103.7	121.4	12.0	143.2	P	👫	🚰
Hartsburg	114.1	111.0	10.4	153.6	P	👫	
Providence	126.0	99.1	11.9	165.5	P	👫	
McBaine	130.0	95.1	15.9	169.5	P	👫	
Rocheport	138.8	86.3	8.8	178.3	P	👫	
New Franklin	148.7	76.4	9.9	188.2	P	👫	🚰
Katy Roundhouse				188.0			⛺
Boonville	152.3	72.8	3.6	191.8	P	👫	
Prairie Lick	197.0						
Pilot Gorve	163.8	61.3	11.5	203.3	P	👫	
Cliff City	175.9	49.2	12.1	215.4	P		
Sedalia	183.6	37.5	11.7	227.1	P	👫	
Green Ridge	199.7	25.4	12.1	239.2	P	👫	
Windsor	208.5	16.6	8.8	248.0	P	👫	
Calhoun	216.0	9.1	7.5	255.5	P	👫	🚰
Clinton	225.1	0	9.1	264.6	P	👫	🚰

Katy Trail State Park (continued)

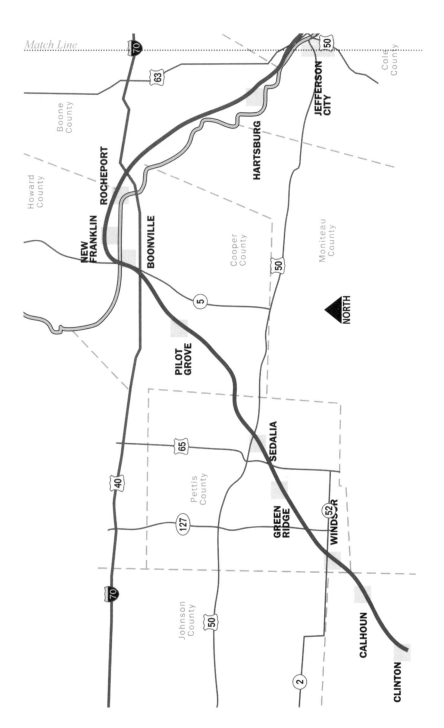

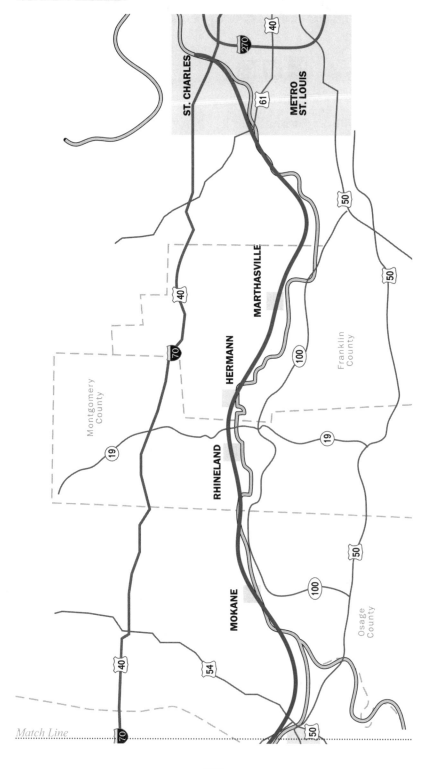

Knob Noster State Park

Trail Uses	🚵 🏃 ⛺
Vicinity	Warrensburg
Trail Length	7 miles
Surface	Natural, groomed
County	Johnson

Trail Notes Only the 7 mile McAdoo Trail of the 7 trails in Knob Noster State Park is open to mountain bikers and equestrians, and is identified with yellow arrows. The trail is mostly flat and will take you through both bottomland and upland forests with a number of creek crossings. You will travel through Christopher Woods, a section of forest that contains the oldest stand of continuous timber within the park. You can cross Clearfork Creek by using an old iron bridge. After heavy rains there are many areas on the trail that hold water. This can be a very rugged trail due to standing water conditions and horse hoof prints.

The 3,567 acre park provides an interesting mixture of prairie, savanna and forest. It lies along both sides of a meandering creek, and contains several small lakes. Facilities include picnic areas, shelters, and campgrounds.

Hiking Trails

Buteo Trail (white arrows), 1+ mile loop – circles Buteo Lake
Clearfork Savanna Trail (blue arrows), half mile loop – tours the Clearfork Savanna
Discovery Trail (green arrows), $\frac{3}{4}$ mile loop – begins in the campground
Hawk Nest Trail (red arrows), $\frac{3}{4}$ mile – shares trail sections with the Buteo and Clearfork Savanna trails
North Loop Trail (yellow arrows), 2 miles – begins in the campground by the first showerhouse
Opossum Hollow Trail (green arrows), 1.5 miles – located at the far end of Redbud Lane

Getting There Knob Noster State Park is located just south of Hwy 50, midway between Sedalia and Warrensburg.
From Kansas City take Hwy 50 east to the Hwy 23/Knob Noster exit. Turn south (right) onto Hwy 23 for about a mile to the main park entrance on the right.

From Springfield take Hwy 65 north to Sedalia, then west (left) on Hwy 50 for about 20 miles to Hwy 23. Turn south (left) on Hwy 23 for a mile to the park entrance on the right.

From Columbia, go west on I-70 to Hwy 65 (Exit 78). Take Hwy 65 south to Hwy 50 in Sedalia. Turn west (right) onto Hwy 50 for about 20 miles to Hwy 23. Turn south (left) on Hwy 23 for a mile to the entrance on the right.

Contact	Knob Noster State Park 660-563-2463, 800-334-6946
	873 SE 10th
	Knob Noster, MO 65336

Northern Missouri

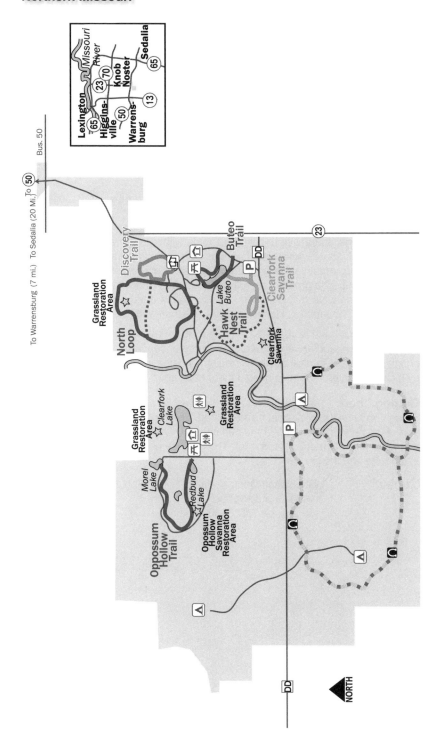

Krug Park

Trail Uses	🚵
Vicinity	St. Joseph
Trail Length	10 miles
Surface	Hard packed dirt
County	Buchanan

Trail Notes   Krug Park is a city park located in northwest St. Joseph. The single-track trail consists of numerous interconnecting loops with some elevation change, a few log crossings, rooted steep sections, and several creek crossings, some with bridges and some without. Some of the short, steep sections may require you to portage. All the trails in the park lead you to the waterfall, a highlight of your ride. The easier and wider trails in the network, identified in green, generally go south from the waterfall. The trails northeast of the waterfall, identified in black, are moderate, while the trails northwest of the waterfall, identified in red, are more difficult.

Much of the trail path is shaded. Facilities include water, restrooms, picnic shelters, a lake, and an amphitheater for summer concerts. There is also a phone available. The trail course is frequently being improved and changed by local bike clubs. A race is hosted there each year.

Getting There   Krug Park is located at Hwy 59 and Karnes Road in St. Joseph. Access the park from Karnes Road. The trailhead is in the northwest part of the park, a little north of the buffalo pens. Look for a stone gate at the far end of the rectangular parking lot. The trail begins from the open area west of the gate and the log cabin.

Contact	St. Joseph Dept. of Parks	816-271-5500
	1920 Grand Avenue	
	St. Joseph, MO 64505	

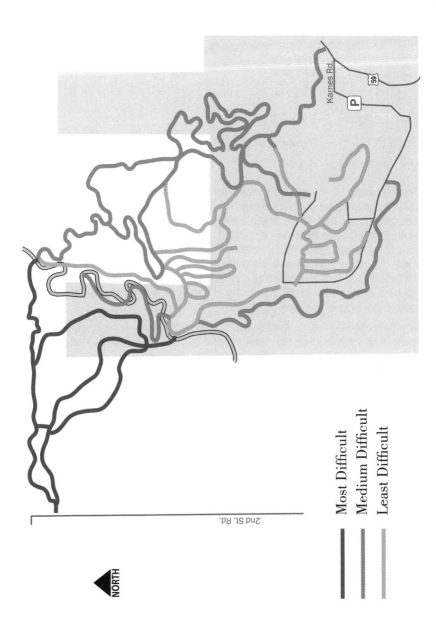

Lick Creek Trail

Trail Uses	🚵 🏃
Vicinity	New London
Trail Length	8.9 miles
Surface	Natural, groomed
County	Ralls

Trail Notes   The Lick Creek Trail is located by Mark Twain Lake, some 15 miles west of New London. The lake can be viewed from many locations on the trail. The surface is single-track, over rocky, hard packed earth. Effort level is moderate to difficult. Habitat types along the trail include upland hardwood, open fields, bottomlands, and limestone bluffs. There are some challenging climbs and descents in and out of the several ravines, but not long climbs. and also a few very tight switchbacks. There are trail markers, but sometimes they are hard to find. High lake levels can cause trails to become impassable.

Ray Behrens Recreation Area is one of the most popular recreation areas at the lake. Facilities include camping, restrooms, water, marina, and picnic area. There are also many hiking trails within this area.

Getting There   From Hannibal, take US 36 west for about 14 miles to Route J. Go south (left) of Route J for 14 miles to Clarence Cannon Dam. Continue across the dam to a parking area and the trailhead across from the US Corps of engineers Ray Behrens Recreation Area. There also is parking access at Hunter/Fisherman Lot 62, and Dusoe Wheelan Recreation Area.

Contact		
	US Army Corps of Engineers 20642 Hwy J Monroe City, MO 63456	573-735-4097
	Mark Twain State Park 20057 State Park Office Road Stoutsville, MO 65283	573-565-3440

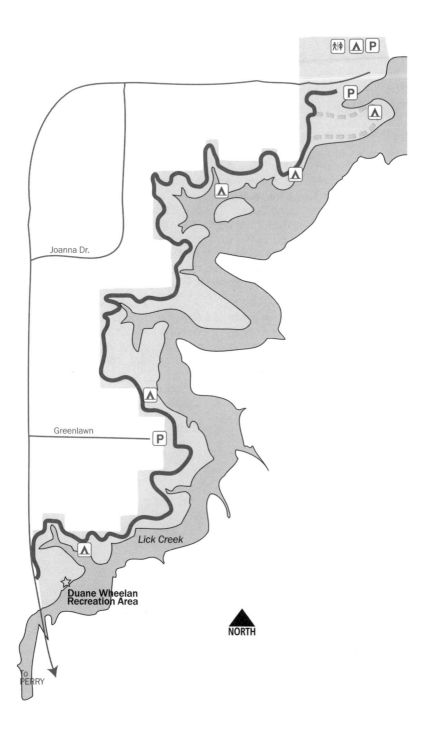

Joanna Dr.

Greenlawn

Lick Creek

Duane Wheelan
Recreation Area

To
PERRY

NORTH

MKT Nature and Fitness Trail

Trail Uses   🚲 🏃 ⛷️

Vicinity   Columbia

Trail Length   8.9 miles

Surface   Crushed limestone

County   Boone

Trail Notes   This 8.9 mile multi-use trail was once a spurline of the Missouri-Kansas-Texas Railroad (MKT), with 4.7 miles in the city of Columbia and 4.2 miles in the Boone County. The city of Columbia received a grant in 1978 for a National Rails-to-Trails conversion. The 10 foot wide trail begins in downtown Columbia in Flat Branch Park. The MKT Trail connects to the 3 mile MU Recreation Trail between Stadium Blvd. and Forum Blvd. The Forum Nature Area Trail winds through 108 acres including a small demonstration wetland habitat, and reconnects to the MKT Trail near Twin Lakes Recreation Area.

The topography is uniform in grade as it slopes from Columbia, southwest to the Missouri River bottoms, where it intersects with the Katy Trail. One of the more unique features located near the intersection of the MKT and Katy Trails is the 4,100 acre Eagle bluffs Conservation Area. There are restrooms and drinking fountains at the Stadium and Forum. The trail landscape is representative of the natural streams and woodlands found in Central Missouri with a wide variety of flora and wildlife.

Trail Access Locations	Parking
Flat Branch Park	Yes
101 S. 4th Street at Cherry St.	Yes
501 S. Providence Road	No
Stadium Blvd. MLK Parking Lot	Yes
2701 Forum Blvd.	Yes
Twin Lakes Recreation Area	Yes
3662 Scott Blvd.	Yes
McBaine Road at the Katy Trail	Yes

Contact   Columbia Parks & Recreation   573-874-7460
1 S. 7th Street
Columbia, MO 65201

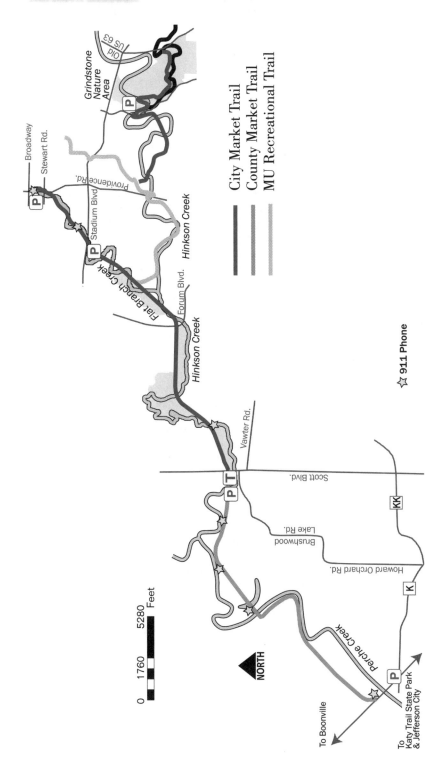

City Market Trail
County Market Trail
MU Recreational Trail

☆ 911 Phone

Grindstone Nature Area

Old US 63

Broadway
Stewart Rd.
Providence Rd.
Stadium Blvd
Flat Branch Creek
Forum Blvd.
Hinkson Creek

Vawter Rd.
Scott Blvd.
Brushwood Lake Rd.
Howard Orchard Rd.
KK
K
Perche Creek

To Boonville
To Katy Trail State Park & Jefferson City

NORTH

0   1760   5280   Feet

Rock Bridge Memorial State Park

Trail Uses	🚵 🏃 🎧
Vicinity	Columbia
Trail Length	13 miles
Surface	Natural
County	Boone

Trail Notes   The six loops of trail making up this trail system generally take you over easy terrain. The effort level varies from easy to moderate. The park's topography, known as "karst", was formed over millions of years by the action of water percolating through the limestone in the park. As water dissolved the limestone, it created sinkholes, caves, underground streams, and springs. Special attractions of this 2,273 acre park include the Devil's Icebox, a huge double sinkhole, where you can pass both under and over the rock or even take the opportunity to explore Connor's Cave. Another is the section of a cave roof that remained after the surrounding portions fell, forming a large natural bridge.

Spring Brook Trail – a 2.5 mile loop that begins from the picnic shelter and Devil's Icebox parking lots. The trail winds through woods and old fields and along small brooks. At the eastern crossing of Femme Creek, a footbridge provides a dry crossing, but the western crossing lacks a bridge. Spring Brook is signed with red arrows.

Sinkhole Trail – a 1.5 mile loop beginning at the Devil's Icebox parking lot and follows an old road through historic Pierpont and continues up a forested valley to a ridge top of old field dotted with sinkholes. A spur connects with the Grassland Trail parking lot, and there is a connector route shortening the loop. Sinkhole Trail is signed with green arrows.

High Ridge Trail – a 2.3 mile loop signed with blue arrows. The trailhead and parking is located on Rock Quarry Road near its intersection with Hwy 163. The trail climbs to a hilltop and follows a ridge before descending to follow Clear Creek. Surrounding parklands can be seen clearly from the ridge. A white connector trail reduces the distance to a half mile.

Grassland Trail – a 2 mile loop signed with blue arrows. The trailhead and parking is located on Rock Bridge Lane. The terrain is gentle and is marked with scattered wooded sinkholes, whose ponds provide habitat for wetland plants and animals such as salamanders, wood ducks and bur reed. There is a white connector that cuts the loop in half.

Karst Trail – a 1.75 mile loop signed with red arrows. The trail begins near the intersection of Hwy 163 and Fox Lane. The terrain is relatively flat with many scattered sinkhole depressions. Devil's Icebox Cave is located nearby, and is only 100 feet underground. The ride takes you past a large pond, an old barn, and several remnant acres of big bluestem grass. This trail also has a short white connector that cuts the loop in half.

Deer Run Trail – a 2.5 mile loop signed with yellow arrows. It begins from the northern picnic areas, and traverses up and down wooded hills along the park's northwestern boundary. It then descends to the flat bottomlands and runs along the banks of the Little Bonne Femme Creek, where it intersects Spring Brook Trail before looping back to its trailhead. The setting is secluded woods and grassy openings. Beaver and muskrats are sometimes seen along the stream.

Paxton Passage – a 0.5 mile loop that begins at its intersection with Deer Run Trail near the northwestern boundary of the park. The trail actually leaves park property and travels on a strip of land donated by Richard Paxton to the Columbia School District. It can be accessed from the grounds of Rock Bridge Elementary School.

Riding in Rock Bridge Memorial State Park
Photo courtesy of the Missouri Department of Natural Resources

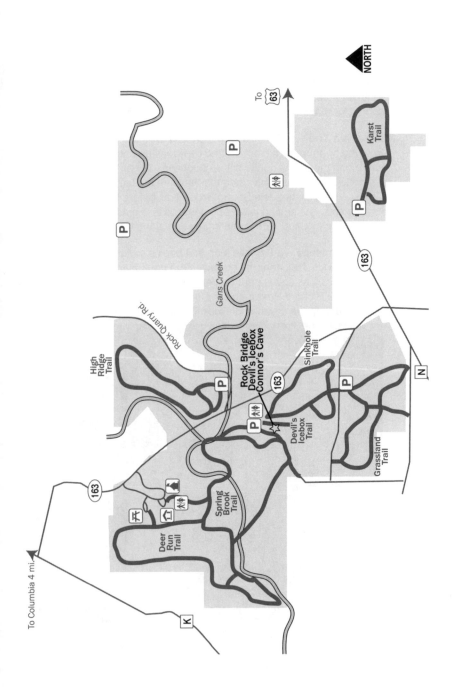

Getting There From Columbia, take US 63 south to MO 163. Turn west (right) to Pierpont. In Pierpont, follow Hwy 163 north for one mile to the large asphalt parking area on the west side of the road, or to the park office a half mile further north.

Contact

Rock Bridge Memorial State Park   573-449-7402
5901 South Hwy 163
Columbia, MO 65203

SYMBOL LEGEND	
🏊	Beach/Swimming
🚲	Bicycle Repair
🏠	Cabin
🅰	Camping
🛶	Canoe Launch
+	First Aid
🅞	Food
GC	Golf Course
?	Information
🛏	Lodging
MF	Multi-Facilities
P	Parking
🌲	Picnic
🧍	Ranger Station
👫	Restrooms
🏠	Shelter
T	Trailhead
🏛	Visitor Center
🚰	Water
🔭	Overlook/Observation

AREA LEGEND	
	City, Town
	Parks, Preserves
	Waterway
	Marsh/Wetland
	Mileage Scale
★	Points of Interest
– –	County/State
🌲	Forest/Woods

TRAIL LEGEND	
▬▬▬	Trail-Biking/Multi
·············	Hiking only Trail
••••••••	Hiking - Multi Use
▬▬▬▬	Snowmobiling only
=========	Planned Trail
— — — —	Alternate Trail
▬▬▬	Road/Highway
+++++++++	Railroad Tracks

St. Joseph Urban Trail

Trail Uses	🚲 🏃 🛼
Vicinity	St. Joseph
Trail Length	10 miles
Surface	Concrete
County	Buchannan

Trail Notes   The Urban Trail is a network of 10' concrete trails and traditional sidewalks linking the neighborhoods of the City of St. Joseph. Much of the opportunity of trail development results from the abandonment of many of the rail lines that once operated within the city. St. Joseph is the fifth largest city in Missouri, and at one time eleven railroads operated here. St. Joseph is also remembered for its link to the Pony Express and the outlaw Jesse James.

Urban Trail System – Distances by Section

Section	Miles
Ferndale to Lover's Lane	0.76
Lover's Lane to Corby Pony	0.78
Corby Pond to Ashland/Noyes	0.48
Ashland/Noyes to Parkway A	1.32
Parkway A to Bartlett Park (Renick)	0.83
Bartlett Park (Renick) to 28th/Commercial	1.20
S.W. Parkway from Mansfield to Hyde Park	0.68
Riverwalk (on Missouri River)	1.17
Former C & N rail line from 36th to Riverside Road	2.00

Planned future development includes:
A section running from S.W. Parkway/22nd Street to Mansfield Road
Extension from Corby Pond along Maple Leaf Parkway to 18th Street
Extension of the Riverwalk further to the north

Contact   St. Joseph Dept. of Public Works & Transportation
816-271-5500
110 Frederick Avenue
St. Joseph, MO 64501

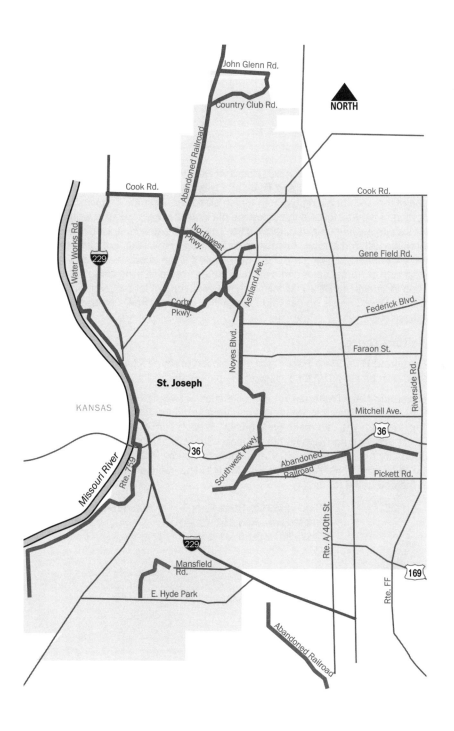

Thousand Hills State Park

Trail Uses	🚴 🚶
Vicinity	Kirksville
Trail Length	11 miles
Surface	Natural
County	Adair

Trail Notes   The 5 mile Thousand Hills Trail traverses both the Big Creek Conservation Area and Thousand Hills State Park and passes through one of the few remaining bigtooth aspen stands in Missouri. The western portion of the trail follows the shoreline of Forest Lake providing opportunities for viewing waterfowl and other wildlife. The trail is signed in a clockwise direction with red arrows. In addition to Thousand Hills Trail, two other great trails for mountain biking are the 3 mile Craig's Cove Loop located on the west side of Forest Lake and a six mile connector trail linking Craig's Cove Loop to Thousand Hills Trail following the south end of forest Lake. The Craig's Cove Loop is an easy ride, while the connector trail is moderate to difficult.

Getting There

Thousand Hills State Park From the junction of Hwy 157 and Hwy 6, go southeast on Hwy 157 for 5 miles to the park entrance.

Thousand Hills Trailhead From the junction of Hwy 157 and Hwy 6, take a right (east) on Hwy 6 to Potter Avenue then turn right. Potter Avenue is the first right turn you can make once on Hwy 6 east. Turn right onto Osteopathy Street and then right again onto Michigan Street. Make a left turn onto Boundary Avenue (Route H). Turn right onto County Road 226 at the sign for the Big Creek Conservation Area on the left. The trailhead and parking lot is at the end of the road.

Contact	Thousand Hills State Park	660-665-6995
	20431 State Hwy 157	
	Kirksville, MO 63501	

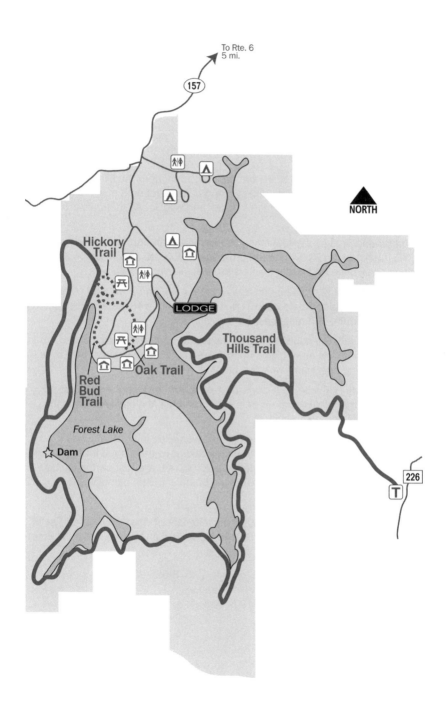

To Rte. 6
5 mi.

157

NORTH

Hickory Trail

LODGE

Thousand Hills Trail

Oak Trail

Red Bud Trail

Forest Lake

Dam

226

T

Wakonda State Park

Trail Uses	🚲 🚶
Vicinity	La Grange
Trail Length	8 miles
Surface	Natural, groomed
County	Lewis

Trail Notes   Located in northeast Missouri, near the Illinois state line, Wakonda State Park has four biking/hiking trails covering 8 miles of scenic views featuring native sand prairies, lakes and wildlife. All the trails are easy to negotiate.

Campground Trail (0.3 miles) takes you from the campground to the trailhead at the main parking lot. During the growing season you should be aware of poison ivy. Prairie and forest animals are also active at this time.

Jasper Lake Trail (2.1 miles) encircles Jasper Lake and a wetland complex, and also connects to Agate Lake Trail. Here signs of wetland animals such as beaver, muskrats, and raccoons are common.

Agate Lake Trail (3.5 miles) encircles the park's largest man-made lake, and connects to both the other hiking trails. Here you will see signs of extensive gravel dredging operations before it became a park.

Peninsula Trail (1.0 mile) is a loop trail, taking you through the sand prairie itself. Look for migrating waterfowl in spring and fall and bird life during the summer in this sparse grassland.

Sand dug up during the gravel excavations was piled in small mounds, created a landscape of rolling sand ridges that have developed into rare sand prairie. The excavation also resulted in a 20,000 square foot swimming beach along Wakonda Lake. The park offers jon boats, canoes, campsites and recreational trailers for rent.

Getting There   From Quincy, Illinois take US 24 west to US 61 at Taylor, Missouri, then north 5 miles on US 61 to Route B (La Grange). Take the inner road south a half mile to the park entrance.

Contact	Wakonda State Park 573-655-2280
	32836 State Park Road
	La Grange, MO 63448

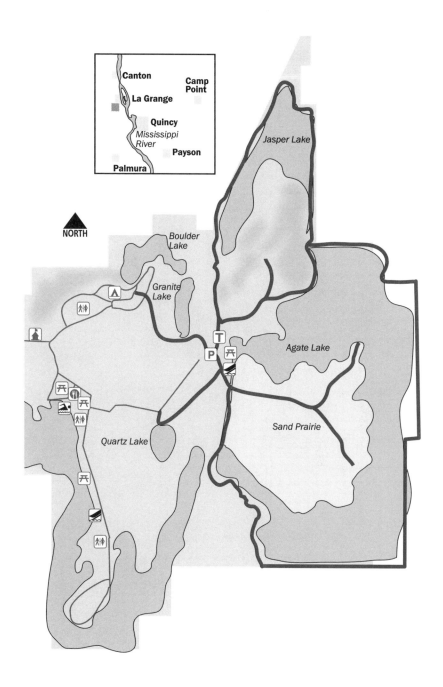

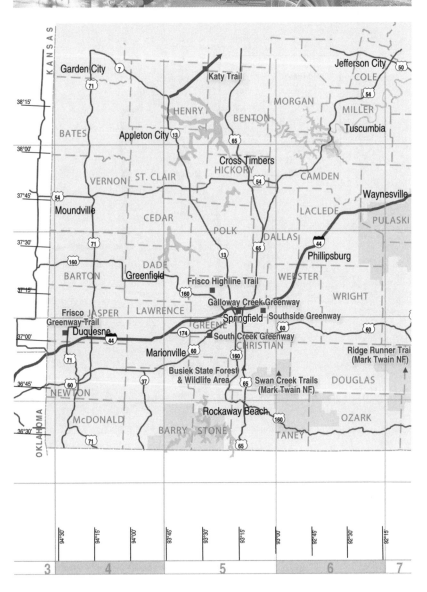

Audubon Trail

Trail Uses

Vicinity   Womack

Trail Length   12 miles

Surface   Natural, groomed

County   Ste. Geneieve

Trail Notes   This is one of the trails in the Mark Twain National
Forest open to mountain biking. Effort level is moderate to difficult, with some
sections requiring you to portage. The surface is single-track and old logging
roads. Expect some steep climbs and descents with loose rock thrown for
good measure on the single-track. By riding the trail clockwise, you'll shortly
cross Bidwell Creek twice before beginning a long climb. The trail is marked
with white trail blazes posted on trees.

The trail is located some 5 miles north of Womack and 15 miles northeast
of Fredericktown. The trailhead and parking is located off Bidwell Creek
Road/FS2199. There are no toilet or drinking water facilities near the trail.
Campsites are located at St. Joe State Park, and Silver Mines Campground,
both west of Farmington.

Getting There   From St. Louis, take Hwy 67 south to Route DD at Knob
Lick. Take Route DD east to Route OO, and then turn south to Route T. At
Route T go east (left) to Bidwell Creek Road/FS 2199. About 5 miles further is
a parking area and the trailhead.

Contact   Greater St. Louis Area Council
                  Boy Scouts of America   314-361-0600
                  4568 West Pine Blvd.
                  St. Louis, MO 63108

                  Potosi Range Station   573-438-5427
                  Mark Twain National Forest

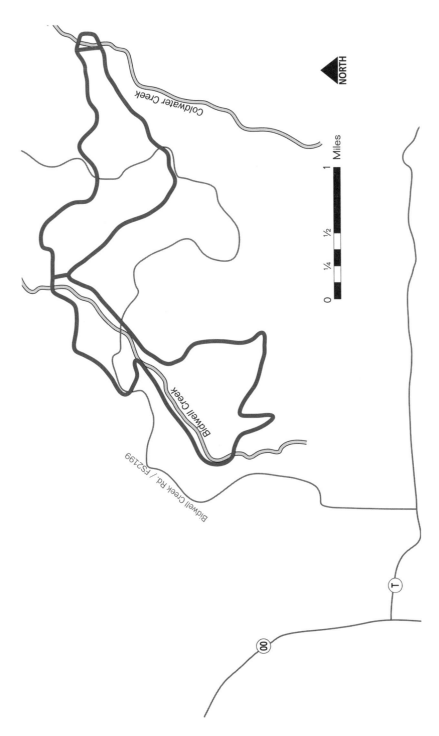

Berryman Trail

Trail Uses	
Vicinity	Potosi
Trail Length	24 miles
Surface	Natural
County	Washington

Trail Notes   The Berryman Trail starts at Berryman Campground, the site of a Civilian Conservation Corps camp, and traverses in a 24 mile loop in scenic Ozark countryside. The trail is single track with technical switchbacks, some located on steep grades. It winds through timbered stands of oak, pine and bottomland hardwoods, climbing switchbacks fashioned from low bottoms to high ridge, glade-like outcroppings and deep forest. The western section of the trail also serves as part of the Courtois Section of the Ozark Trail.

There are mileage markers located at intervals along the trail, starting at Berryman Campground, with numeric values increasing as you proceed clockwise around the loop trail.

Camping is permitted anywhere along the trail. Berryman Campground is located 1 miles north of Hwy 8, about 16 miles west of Potosi and 19 miles east of Steelville. Brazil Creek Campground is located about 6 miles north of Berryman Campground, and can be accessed by way of Forest Roads 2266 and 2265. There are 8 single camping sites, each with a table, sanitary facilities, fire ring and lantern post. There are several picnic sites available with tables and picnic grills, and centrally located vault toilets, but not drinking water.

Getting There   From Potosi, take Hwy 8 west for 16 miles to CR 207, then turn north for about 1.5 miles to Berryman Camp.

Contact   Potosi/Fredericktown Ranger District   573-438-5427
Hwy 8 West
Potosi, MO 63664

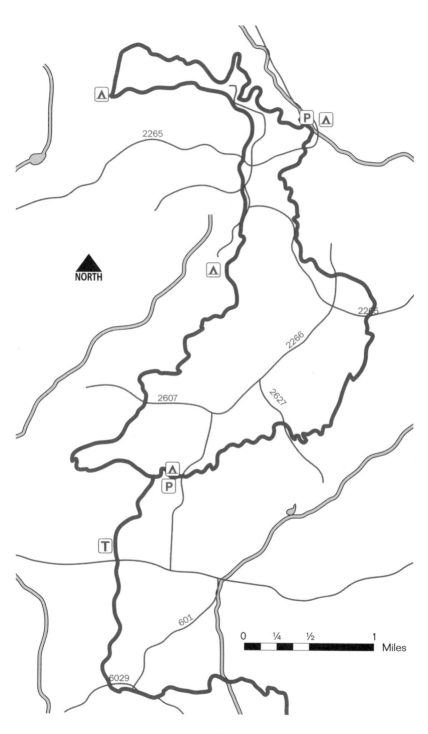

Between the Rivers Trail

Trail Uses   🚲 🚶 🏕

Vicinity   Van Buren

Trail Length   30 miles

Surface   Natural

County   Carter

Trail Notes   This section of the Ozark Trail is located on public land that lies between the Current River and the Eleven Point River and is part of the Mark Twain National Forest. The terrain is typical of most of the Ozarks region, with exposed roots, rocks, gravel, and some sharp turns. Effort level varies from easy to difficult. Your best seasons are spring and fall. During the summer months be prepared for high temperatures, biting insects, and poison ivy. Be advised of the hunting seasons. There are campsites at Big Spring and Watercress Spring Recreation Area.

The northern trailhead is on Hwy 60, west of Van Buren. From there the trail heads southwest to Forest Road #3152 near Hurricane Creek. It generally leads south for the first 13 miles, winding through numerous small tributaries that feed the Current River. From Big Barren Creek, the trail heads west along the north prong of Cedar Bluff Creek. then climbs gently out of Cedar Bluff Creek drainage and crosses a major ridge that divides the Current River watershed and the Eleven Point River watershed. The remaining 8.5 miles of the trail continues southwest following Gold Mine Hollow, the ridge above Kelly Hollow, and Fox Hollow before ending on Forest Service Road #3152 above Hurricane Creek.

Getting There   From Van Buren, go 3.5 miles west on Hwy 60. Parking is available at Hwy 60 and Sinking Creek Lookout Tower, west of Hwy J.

Contact   Mark Twain National Forest   573-364-4621
                  401 Fairgrounds Road
                  Rolla, MO 65401

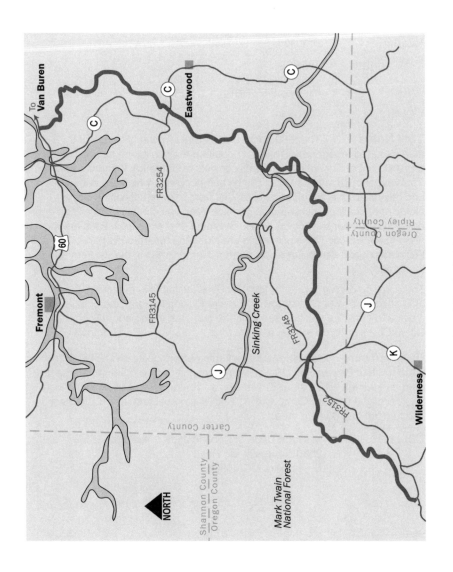

Busiek State Forest

Trail Uses

Vicinity   Branson

Trail Length   14 miles

Surface   Natural, groomed

County   Christian

Trail Notes   The 2,505 acre Busiek State Forest is typical of this area's rugged topography. This is a popular mountain biking destination for bicyclists out of Springfield. The trail consists of single-track and fire roads. You'll experience some serious climbs and descents, which are both steep and technical. Overall, effort level ranges from easy to difficult. There are plenty of rocks, logs, ticks and chiggers to keep you company. Mornings and evenings are your best riding times. The more challenging sections are the hills east of US 65. The easier rides are along the forest roads paralleling Woods Fork and Camp Creek, or north of Camp Creek in the western end of the forest.

There are no drinking water or toilet facilities available in the forest. Ozark or Branson are your closest towns if you're looking for food and drink, and a place to bunk. As you can see from the map, the trails generally parallel Camp Creek and you are never more than a couple of miles from US 65.

Getting There   Located 22 miles south of Springfield on US 65 or 20 miles north of Branson on US 65. From Springfield, take US 65 to a gravel road on your left with a small brown sign as you're descending down a long hill, just a little north of Camp Creek. Take this gravel road to a T intersection and turn left to a parking area.

Contact   Missouri Dept. of Conservation   417-895-6880
2630 North Mayfair Road
Springfield, MO 65803

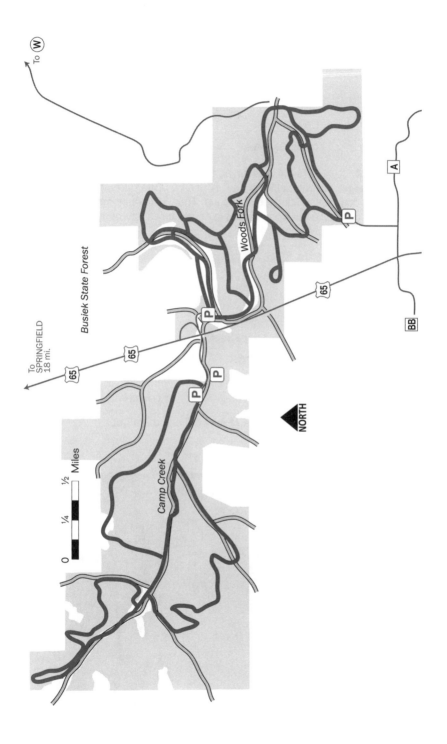

Cape LaCroix Recreation Trail

Trail Uses   🚲 🚶 ⛸

Vicinity   Cape Girardeau

Trail Length   4.4 miles

Surface   Paved

County   Cape Girardeau

Trail Notes   This 4.4 mile paved trail provides a travel route from the Osage Community Centre across the City of Cape Girardeau to the Shawnee Park Sports complex at Minnesota Avenue. The trail is open from 6 am to 11 pm. The path includes white stripes in 1/10th mile increments and yellow stripes in $\frac{1}{4}$ miles increments.

Distance Increments

Route W to Hoppe Road	1.0 miles
Hopper Road to Rodney Street	1.1 miles
Rodney Street to Independence Street	0.4 miles
Independence Street to William Street	0.3 miles
William Street to Bloomfield Street	0.5 miles
Bloomfield Street to Brink Street	0.2 miles
Brink Street to Shawnee Park	1.0 miles

Contact   Cape Girardeau Parks & Recreation Dept.
573-335-5421

Council Bluffs Lake Trail

Trail Uses	🚵 🚶
Vicinity	Potosi
Trail Length	13 miles
Surface	Natural, groomed
Counties	Iron, Washington

Trail Notes   This 13 mile trail circles the shoreline of Council Bluffs Lake on the Big River. The lake was formed by damming the Big River. It's one of the most scenic mountain bike trails in Missouri. The trail is mostly single track except for an old logging road and a half mile gravel road. The single track is challenging, technical, and rocky. Turns can be sharp, with steep descents, although by starting off clockwise the first two miles of the trail are easy until you cross the Telleck Branch of the Ozark Trail. If you choose, you then can access the Ozark Trail by taking the spur trail for a quarter mile from just before you cross the footbridge at the branch.

There is a parking fee when you get to the parking lot. After paying the fee ride toward the beach, go past a sign to the right of the parking lot stating no motor vehicles allowed past this point. The trail heads downhill to ride counterclockwise, or you can go clockwise by taking paved & gravel roads for a short distance and entering the trail before the gate. There are toilets and a picnic area located at the trailhead. Water is available at the campground. A picnic area, toilets and cold-water showers are also available at the swimming beach.

Getting There   From St. Louis take Hwy 21 to Potosi. From Potosi, take Hwy 8 west for a quarter mile to Hwy P heading south. Hwy P turns into Hwy DD as it crosses Hwy C. Continue south on Hwy DD for another 8 miles to the Council Bluffs Lake Recreation Area on the left.

Contact	Potosi/Fredericktown Ranger District	573-438-5427
	Hwy 8 West	
	Potosi, MO 63664	

Southern Missouri

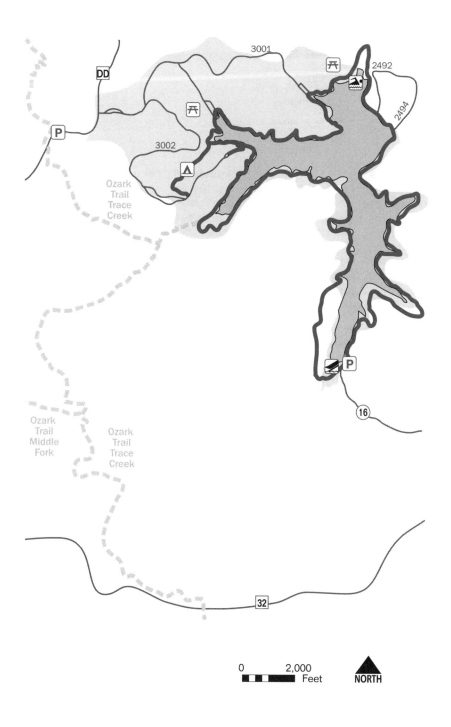

3001

DD

2492

2494

3002

Ozark
Trail
Trace
Creek

P

3002

⛺

P

16

Ozark
Trail
Middle
Fork

Ozark
Trail
Trace
Creek

32

0   2,000
     Feet

NORTH

Eleven Point River Trail

Trail Uses   🚲 🚶 ⛺

Vicinity   Greer

Trail Length   30 miles

Surface   Natural

County   Oregon

Trail Notes   From the FR3152 trailhead, the trail winds along the side slope to Hurricane Creek. These first 10 miles pass through some very rugged slopes and flowages, but with some great views of Eleven Point valley. From the Greer Recreation area 10 miles out, the trail parallels the Eleven Point River on its way to McCormack Lake. At 13 miles out there is a spur leading to McCormick Lake. As you continue west, the trail winds through more rugged terrain and a couple more sightings of the river. At about 20 miles out, the trail passes next to Bockman Spring, a part of the Spring Creek Flowage. The last 10 miles of the trail are in the Spring Creek flowage. The trail ends at FR 4155.

Getting There   From Winona, take Hwy 19 south for 15 miles to FS 3152. Go east some six miles to the trailhead, or take Hwy 19 south for 13 miles to FR 3155. Go west on FR3155 for 2 miles to McCormack Road 4155, then north to the trailhead.

From Thomasville, take Hwy 99 north 3.5 miles to FR 3173. Go east on FR3173 for 1.5 miles to FR 4155, then north to the Ozark Trail trailhead.

Contact   Eleven Point River Ranger District Office   573-325-4233
                        Route 1, Box 1908
                        Winona, MO 65588

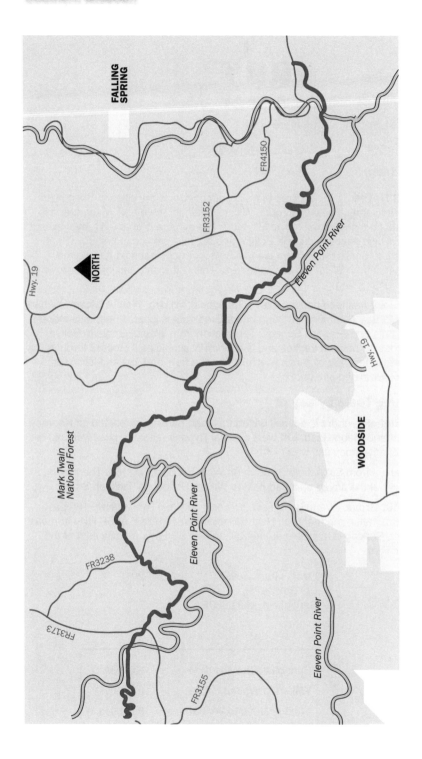

Frisco Highline Trail

Trail Uses	🚲 🚶 ⛷ 🎧
Vicinity	Springfield, Bolivar
Trail Length	36 miles
Surface	Asphalt, crushed stone, dirt
Counties	Greene, Polk

Trail Notes   This rail-to-trails path connects the cities of Springfield and Bolivar as it passes through Willard, Walnut Grove and Wishart, and is the second longest rail-trail in Missouri. The surface is crushed gravel except for a 1 mile paved section in Bolivar and a 2 mile section in Willard. There is also a 10 mile natural-surface trail built for equestrians paralleling the main trail from Willard to Walnut Grove. This is the only section that allows horseback riding.

There are trailhead parking lots in Springfield, Willard, Walnut Grove, Wishart and Bolivar. A campground and bed & Breakfast is located near mile marker 20, at historic Graydon Springs. The section from Walnut Grove to Bolivar includes 13 railroad trestles and is especially scenic as it crosses through the Ozarks landscape of gentle hills, picturesque farmland, colorful foliage and many rivers and streams.

Getting There by way of

Springfield – there is a small paved trailhead parking lot located on Kearney Street and Eldon Road, just west of West Bypass (about 5 miles west of Hwy 13, take Kearney exit west).

Willard – from Springfield go north on West Bypass/Hwy 160. There is parking at the paved trailhead next to Willard School on Jackson Street.

Walnut Grove – from Springfield, go north on West Bypass/Hwy 160 past Willard, then north (right) on Hwy 123 for about 10 miles. At BB Hwy turn east (right). Parking is available at the trailhead on BB Hwy, a $\frac{1}{4}$ mile east of the traffic light.

Contact   Ozark Greenways   417-864-2015
               PO Box 50733
               Springfield, MO 65805

Springfield to Willard	6.0 miles
Willard to Walnut Grove	10.0 miles
Walnut Grove to Wishart	8.5 miles
Wishart to Bolivar	11.5 miles

Southern Missouri

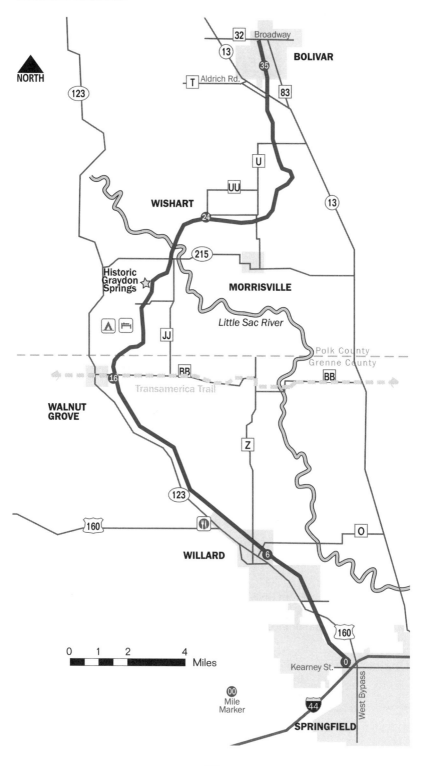

NORTH

BOLIVAR

Broadway
32
13
35
83

T Aldrich Rd.

123

U

13

UU

WISHART

24

215

Historic
Graydon
Springs

MORRISVILLE

Little Sac River

Polk County
Grenne County

JJ

RB

BB

Transamerica Trail

WALNUT
GROVE

16

Z

123

160

O

WILLARD

6

160

0   1   2   4
                       Miles

160

0
Kearney St.

West Bypass

00
Mile
Marker

44

SPRINGFIELD

Kaintuck Trail

Trail Uses	🚵 🏃 ⋂
Vicinity	Rolla
Trail Length	24 miles
Surface	Gravel and dirt roads, natural
County	Phelps

Trail Notes   The 24 mile Kantuck Trail is located south of the Mill Creek Recreation Area and is part of the Mark Twain National Forest. The trail is a network of 9 interconnecting, generally easy riding loops. The surface varies from gravel forest roads, to old logging roads and single-track. The route passes a 175 foot cave, which is a natural tunnel with limestone walls. The terrain is gently rolling, with several stream crossings, and a few steep single-track areas.

The Acorn Section follows an old logging road west of Kaintuck Hollow for 4 miles.

The Butterfly Section takes you down through cedars, then over a streambed covered with large, mossy rocks.

The Mushroom Section connects the Acorn and Pine Tree and Pine Tree sections.

The Pine Tree Section runs parallel to a gravel road connecting Mill Creek Recreation Area with Hwy T, and is about 3 miles long.

The Squirrel Section connects to the Oak Leaf Section, near the Natural Bridge and tunnel.

The Deer Track Section starts out as a wide track, then loops southwest, after passing a small lily pond, to Wilkins Spring and back to Acorn.

The Cardinal Section follows an old double-track on the ridge top for about a half mile, and then branches to the east before descending into Kaintuck Hollow.

The Grouse Section runs from the Wilkins Spring intersection with the Acorn Section.

Getting There   From Rolla, take I-44 west to Hwy T (Exit 179). South on Hwy T for 2 miles, then go right on Hwy P for 2.8 miles. At FS 7550 turn left for 2.3 miles to the entrance road at your left leading to a parking area and the trailhead.

Contact	Mark Twain National Forest	573-364-4621
	401 Fairgrounds Road	
	Rolla, MO 65041	

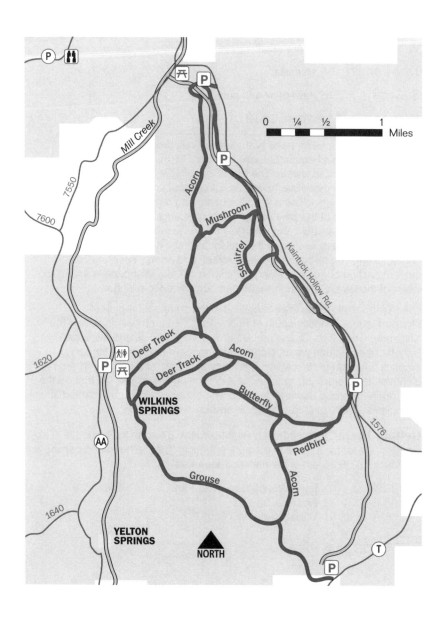

Lake Wappapello State Park

Trail Uses	🚴 🚶 ⛺
Vicinity	Poplar Bluff
Trail Length	15 miles
Surface	Hard pack dirt, gravel
Counties	Wayne, Butler

Trail Notes The Lake Wappapello Trail, designed for all-terrain bicycling, hiking and equestrian use, wanders 15 miles through varied and rugged Ozark upland terrain. The trail is identified with yellow markers. The effort level is moderate to difficult. Directional arrows for the trail point you counterclockwise. There is trailhead parking on Route 172, less than a quarter mile west of the park office. The trail is single-track with some short sections of double-track, and a surface that is generally hard pack dirt or gravel. The western section of the trail loop climbs and descends between the ridges, taking you through hardwood forest, and across several streams. The eastern section brings you along the shores of Lake Wappapello and hilltop views of the lake. Other trails in the park are limited to hiking.

Lake Wappapello State Park is nestled in the southeast region of Missouri, about 25 miles south of Poplar Bluff. Indian tribes, including the Shawnee, Cherokee, Osage and Delaware, originally settled the area. Park facilities include water, picnic areas, modern restrooms, laundry facilities, campgrounds, cabins, a swimming beach, and boating. There is a convenience store just outside the entrance on Route 172. All trails in the park open for public use are identified with entrance signs and marked at intersections with colored directional arrows.

Getting There From Poplar Bluff take Hwy 67 north to Route 172. Take Route 172 east for 8 miles to the park entrance. The trailhead and parking are on Route 172 just west of the park headquarters.

Contact	Lake Wappapello State Park	573-297-3232
	Route 2, Box 102	
	Williamsville, MO 63967	

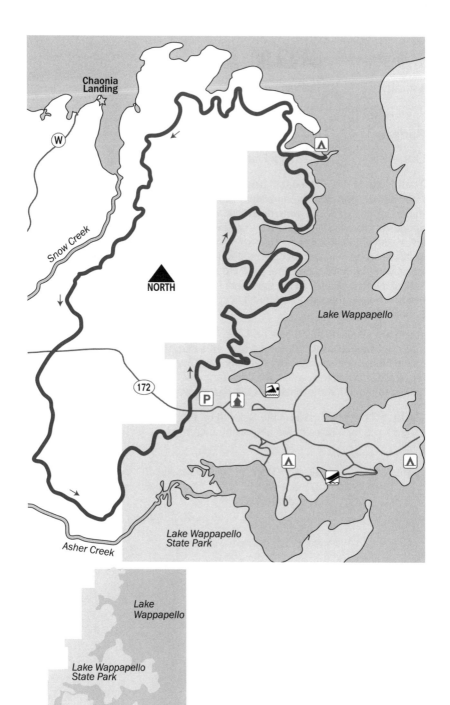

Meramec Conservation Area

Trail Uses	
Vicinity	Sullivan
Trail Length	10 miles
Surface	Old forest roads, double-track
Counties	Crawford, Franklin, Washington

Trail Notes   The 4,045 acre Meramec Conservation Area features forested hills and hollows, a trail that winds along the Meramec River, climbs to panoramic overlooks, and meanders along occasional streams, past springs and caves. While there you can visit an abandoned fire lookout. Effort level is easy to moderate, with a few climbs that may require walking. The trail surface is a combination of old forest roads and double-track. The east side takes you through a pine grove on a carpet of pine needles. The old Reedville schoolhouse is located at the northeast corner of the ride. Remember that this is an equestrian trail, and that biking is not allowed on the Old Reedville School Hiking Trail

There are pit toilets at the trailhead, but no water. Meramec State Park, 1 mile northwest and just across the river, has campsites, picnic areas, a rustic dining lodge, general store, a boat ramp, and canoe, raft, and inner tube rentals. If you visit the park, don't pass up the Visitor Center with its 3,500-gallon aquarium, and consider a cave tour as well.

Getting There   Take I-44 to Sullivan off Exit 226. From Sullivan, go east on Hwy 185 for 4 miles to the gravel entrance road on the left at the bottom of a hill.

Contact	Missouri Dept. of Conservation 573-468-3335
	375 S. Hwy 185
	Sullivan, MO 63080

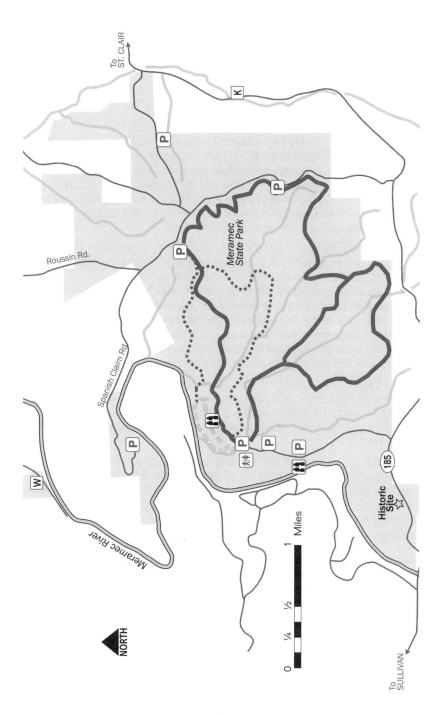

Ridge Runner Trail

Trail Uses

Vicinity   West Plaines

Trail Length   22 miles

Surface   Natural, groomed

County   Howell

Trail Notes   The Ridge Runner Trail is 22 miles long, extending from Noblett Lake in the north to the North Fork Recreation Area to the south. The trail is designed and maintained for mountain biking, hiking and equestrian use. There are also two hiking loops: an 8 mile trail around Noblett Lake, and a 12 mile trail in the Steam Mill Hollow area. This is a challenging trail in a remote, wilderness setting. Effort level is moderate to difficult. The surface is narrow single-track and abandoned logging roads.

There are long climbs and fast descents scattered throughout the trail, and occasions when you will have to portage your bike. The North Fork Loop is moderate, but can be an especially difficult hill if you take it counterclockwise. There is a steep descent from the ridge above down to the stream below, although it does provide a long scenic ride. The Norblett Loop also has many steep and rocky climbs and descents. The trails are maintained in the spring and fall, but vegetation growth near stream crossings and intersecting woods roads may make the trail hard to follow. The trails are marked with grey plastic diamonds tacked to trees every few hundred feet.

Drinking water is available from April 15 to October 15 at the North Fork and Noblett lake recreation areas. Carrying your own drinking water, as well as a map and compass is recommended. Camping is not permitted within a 100 feet of the trails, ponds, bluffs or caves. There are campgrounds at North Fork and Noblett Lake

The landscape varies from gently rolling to very steep terrain with rock outcrops and bluffs. This part of the Missouri Ozarks is known for it beauty and limestone Karst topography. The vegetation along the trail is diverse and includes oak, hickory, pine, and bottomland forests. Native wildflowers, and flowering dogwood are abundant. Wild turkey, and white-tailed deer may be seen on occasion.

Getting There   The north trailhead is in the Norblett Lake Recreation Area. From Willow Springs, take Hwy 76 west for 8 miles to Hwy 181. Go south on Hwy 181 for 1.5 miles to Hwy AP. Turn left on Hwy AP and continue for 3 miles to the recreation area entrance. You'll find the trailhead next to the campground.

The south trailhead is in the North Fork Recreation Area on the White River. From West Plain, take Hwy CC west for 18 miles to the campground, where you'll find Ridge Runner trailhead sign and parking nearby.

Contact   Will Spring Ranger District   417-469-3155
PO Box 99
Will Springs, MO 65793

Ridge Runner Trail Trailheads as referenced on the map
From/to the Noblett Lake Recreation Area

0/0/22.0 mile Noblett Lake Creation Area

The Noblett trailhead is on FR 8576 near the Recreation Area. The lake was created in the late 1930's as a CCC project.

3.3/18.7 miles Horton

Several springs can be found along the trail. Galloway Springs is a short walk to the east of the trail. Many of the old roads that remain from the lumber town of Horton either cross or parallel the trail. Tombstones in Horton Cemetery near the trailhead testify to a plague in 1902.

8.0/14.0 miles Blue Hole Hollow

Misty mornings gave these hills a bluish cast, prompting early settlers to call the area Blue Hole. Prairie grasses and flowers are now common in the area, resulting from large wildfires. The Ozark Trail ties into the Ridge Runner from here south to the North Fork Trailhead.

10.5/11.5 miles   Hwy 14

The trail crosses Hwy 14 at this point, but the trailhead is not developed.

13.0/9.0 miles Hay Hollow

The trailhead can be accessed from Hwy 14 by turning south onto FR 769, as well as from the Ridge Runner Trail, where it drops down a hillside into the normally dry Tabor Creek bottom. Parking, primitive camping and picnicking is available.

19.0/3.0 miles Steam Mill Hollow

This area features a deep hollow with spring branches entering the North Fork of the White River. A portion of the trail overlooks the river.

22.0/0.0 miles North Fork

This trailhead is located at the North Fork Recreation Area. Facilities include campgrounds, picnic areas, a canoe launch, toilets, and drinking water. Blue Springs and the Devil's Backbone Wilderness are adjacent to the trailhead.

12.1 miles   North Fork Loop

Recommended for hikers and equestrians. The loop leaves the Recreation Area and crosses Hwy CC, passing through dense hardwood forest, then parallels the North Fork of the White River. After leaving the river, the trail continues over scenic ridges and hollows before completing the loop back at the North Fork Recreation Area.

Ridge Runner Trail (continued)

Location	Mileage		Facilities
Noblett Recreation Area	0.0	22.0	Parking, Water, Restrooms, Picnic
Horton Trailhead	3.3	18.7	Parking
Blue Hold Trailhead	8.0	14.0	Parking, Picnic
Wrangler Trailhead	9.6	12.8	
Hay Hollow Trailhead	13.0	9.0	Parking, Camping
Steam Mill Hollow	19.0	3.0	
North Fork Recreation Area	22.0	0.0	Water, Camping, Parking, Restrooms, Picnic

SYMBOL LEGEND

- Beach/Swimming
- Bicycle Repair
- Cabin
- Camping
- Canoe Launch
- First Aid
- Food
- Golf Course
- Information
- Lodging
- Multi-Facilities
- Parking
- Picnic
- Ranger Station
- Restrooms
- Shelter
- Trailhead
- Visitor Center
- Water
- Overlook/ Observation

AREA LEGEND

- City, Town
- Parks, Preserves
- Waterway
- Marsh/Wetland
- Mileage Scale
- Points of Interest
- County/State
- Forest/Woods

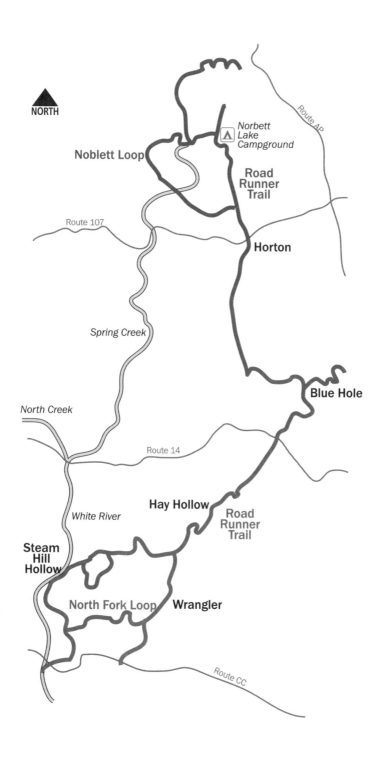

NORTH

Norbett Lake Campground

Noblett Loop

Road Runner Trail

Route AP

Route 107

Horton

Spring Creek

North Creek

Blue Hole

Route 14

Hay Hollow

Road Runner Trail

White River

Steam Hill Hollow

North Fork Loop

Wrangler

Route CC

Southside Greenways

Trail Uses

	South Creek	Galloway Creek
Vicinity	Springfield	
County	Greene	
Trail Length	8 miles	5 miles
Surface	Concrete	Asphalt
	Crushed gravel	crushed gravel

Trail Notes   **South Creek Greenway**   The starting point is the McDaniel Trailhead at Sunset & National streets. There are currently over 8 miles of trail connecting to Nathanael Green Park, the Japanese Gardens, Close Memorial Park, Horton Smith Golf Course, Carver Middle School and local neighborhoods. Parking is available at the Natanael Greene Park and the Volunteer Nature Trail trailhead. The 1 mile Volunteer Nature Trail has a wood-chipped surface and joins the paved greenway in southwest Springfield, near the Southwest Water Treatment Plant. The trail will eventually connect from the McDaniel Park Trailhead to Wilson's Creek National Battlefield. There is a pedestrian and bicycling overpass at Kansas Expressway, and an underpass at Campbell Street.

Galloway Creek Greenway   There are currently over 5 miles of trail connecting Pershing Middle School at Seminole & Lone Pine to Sequiota Park and to the Springfield Conservation Nature Center. The trail winds under Highway 60 and 65 and then over the old iron James River bridge. Other connections include Springfield Lake, Galloway Village, Galloway Station Restaurant, and several neighborhoods. Parking is available at Pershing Middle School, Sequiota Park, the south end of Lone Pine Avenue, and at the old Iron James River Bridge. Bikes are not allowed on the Nature Center trails. The first mile of the James River Greenway connects to Galloway Creek Greenway, west of the Old Iron Bridge.

Contact   Ozark Greenways
471-864-2015
PO Box 50733
Springfield,
MO 65805

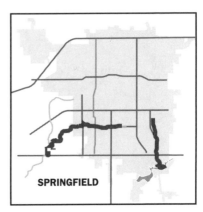

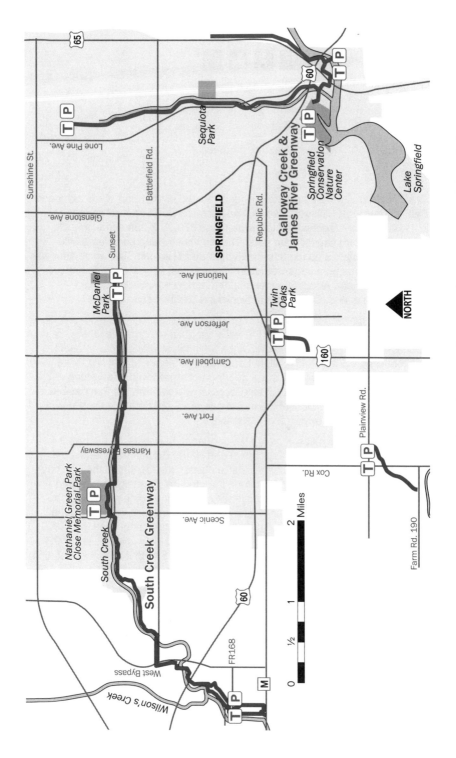

St. Joe State Park

Trail Uses	🚵 🚲 🚶 ⛸ ⛏	
Vicinity	Farmington, Park Hills	
	Surfaced	**Mountain**
Trail Length	13.8 miles	15 miles
Surface	Paved Natural, groomed	
County	St. Francois	

Trail Notes   St. Joe State Park is located in the heart of the old "Lead Belt" of southeast Missouri. The St. Joe Minerals Corp. ceased operations in 1972 and donated the land to the state in 1976. At 8,238 acres, this is Missouri's third largest state park. The old mine milling complex is still standing and makes up the Missouri Mines State Historic Site, which houses a museum featuring a large collection of geological specimens and antique mining equipment. About 25 percent of the park is honeycombed with underground mines. Camping and picnicking facilities are available.

There are approximately 15 miles of mountain bike trails that are shared with hikers and horses. Some of the trails are quite rocky, while others are good earthen trails. Some portions of the trails follow along small streams. Red Trail is a 7.5 mile loop trail that originates and ends at Pimville Road. While not too technical there is a wide range of terrain with a few steep sections. Lakeview Trail is a 1.5 mile loop accessible from the Pim day-use or Monsanto Lake area. Most of the trail is earthern, and both level and steep, except for a partially paved .2 mile section.

There are also 13.8 miles of paved trails, open to bicyclists, hikers, skate boarders and roller skaters. Brankshire and Harris Branch trailheads are located along Pimville Road. Other trail accesses are located at the Pim day-use area, Missouri Mines State Historic Site and the Farmington trailhead. The terrain ranges from level to fairly steep hills along some portions of the trail. The section of trail north of Pimville Road is 8 miles in length, and the section south of Pimville Road is 3 mile long. The spur connecting the Pim day-use area to the bicycle trail is .6 miles long and fairly level, as is the 0.5 mile spur connecting Missouri Mines State Historic Site to the northern portion of the trail. The newest section of the tail connecting the trail at about the 1.5 mile marker to the Farmington trailhead is 1.7 miles long.

Getting There   From St. Louis, take I-55 south to Festus and exit at Hwy 67. Take Hwy 67 south toward Park Hills and Farmington until it intersects with Hwy 32. Follow Hwy 32 west to the park entrance on the left.

From Farmington, take Hwy 67 north to Park Hills, then left on Hwy 32 west to the park entrance on the left.

Once you enter the park take Pimville Road to the park office or the bicycle staging area just to the right.

Contact   St. Joe State Park   573-431-1069
           2800 Pimville Road
           Park Hills, MO 63601

NORTH

0	4,000	8,000

Feet

Swan Lake Trail

Trail Uses	🚵 🏃 🎧
Vicinity	Chadwick
Trail Length	21 miles
Surface	Fire/gravel roads, single-track
County	Christian

Trail Notes　The Swan Creek lies within Mark Twain National Forest. It's a scenic wooded area with some big hills and several streams. The trail system was built for equestrians, but is open to mountain biking and hiking. Here you'll find lots of rocks, roots, some fast turns, steep hills and depressions from horse's hoofs. Overall effort level is moderate, with many of the trails offering easy riding. You will almost certainly have to portage some of the single-track.

The Forest Service built the Bar K Wrangler Camp in 1992, and marked the trails with numbers, although they kept the unique names assigned by the equestrian developers of the trail system years before. The trails were given such titles as "Beer Can Alley", "Moonshine Hollow", and "Tin Top Ridge". The main entrance is the Bar K Wrangler Camp on the west bank of Swan Creek, off FR 533, although most mountain bikers seem to prefer the entrance off Hwy UU on the eastern side of the recreation area. The Bar K Wrangle Camp area does offer picnic table, toilets, grills, and or course, hitching posts.

Some of the sections generally preferred by mountain bikers:

"Tin Top", off Hwy UU, and an alternate trailhead entrance. After 1.5 miles the trail forks off to the "Beer Can Alley" section.

The "Math Branch" section is in the northern park of the territory and follows a branch of Swan Creek.

Parallel to "Tin Top" is the "Shoo Fly" section and a spur branching off to link back to "Tin Top".

The "Patterson Hollow" section on the east side connects to the "Tin Top" and "Whoppin' Willie" trail.

Getting There　From Springfield, take Hwy 65 south to the town of Ozark. Take Hwy 14 (the 2nd Ozark exit) east past Sparta to Oldfield, where Hwy 14 forks. Take the right fork (Hwy 125) through the town of Chadwick for 6 miles to the main Swan Creek entrance (FR 533) on your left. Park in the bottoms near the creek.

To get to the eastern side of Swan Creek, take the left fork off Hwy 14 (Hwy T) east to Hwy UU. Take Hwy UU south to FF 6107 on the right.

Contact	Ava Ranger District	417-683-4428
	PO Box 188	
	Ava, MO 65608	

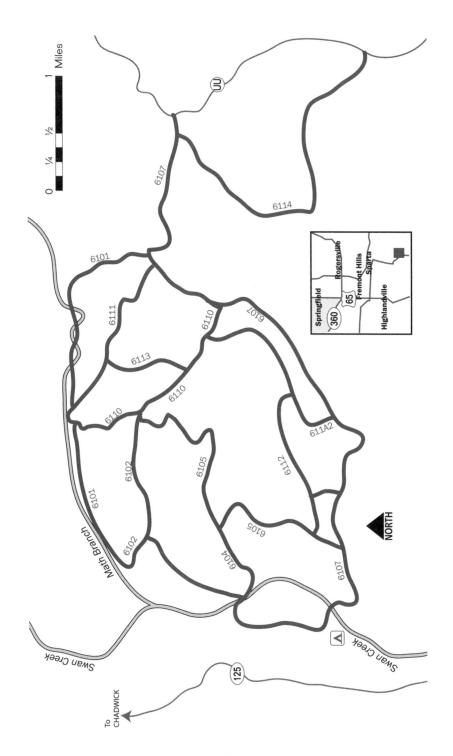

Southern Missouri

Adventure Cycling Association
PO Box 8308
Missoula, Mt 59807
406-721-1776

Bicycle Federation of America
1818 R St. NW
Washington, DC 20009
202-332-6986

Cyclists of Greater St. Louis
PO Box 13206
St. Louis, MO 63157
314-532-7496

Dept. of Natural Resources
Division of State Parks
PO Box 176
Jefferson City, MO 65102
800-334-6946

Division of Tourism
PO Box 1055
Jefferson City, MO 65102
673-751-4133

Earth Riders
7405 N. Woodland Ave.
Gladstone, MO 64118
816-231-0996
www.earthriders.org

Greater Kansas City Bicycle
Federation
http://kcbikefed.org

Hostelling International/AYH
7187 Manchester Road
St. Louis, MO 63143
314-644-4660
www.gatewayhiayh.org

International Mountain Bicycling
Association (IMBA)
PO Box 7578
Boulder, CO 80396
303-545-9011

Katy Central Association
PO Box 872
Columbia, MO 65205
888-441-2023

League of American Bicyclists
190 W. Ostend St., Ste 120
Baltimore, MD 21230
410-539-3399

Mark Twain National Forest
401 Fairgrounds Road
Rolla, MO 65401
573-364-4621

Midwest Mountain Bike Patrol
www.earthriders.com/MMBP/

Missouri Bicycle Federation
PO Box 104871
Jefferson City, MO 65110
573-636-4488
www.mobikefed.org

Missouri Dept of Conservation
41 South Central, 7th Floor
Clayton, MO 63105
314-889-2874

Missouri State Parks Foundation
www.missouriparksfoundation.org

Moonlight Ramble
St. Louis
www.bikeride.com

National Off-Road Bicycle
Association (NORBA)
One Olympic Plaza
1750 E Boulder Street
Colorado Springs, CO 80909
719-578-4717

St. Louis Regional Bicycle Federation
http://stlbikefed.org

Trail Advocacy
2 S Grim Ct
Kirksville, MO 63501

U.S. Army Corps of Engineers
Rte 2, Box A
Wappapello, MO 63966
314-222-8234

Bicycle Fun Club
PO Box 1564
Maryland Heights, MO 63043
314-739-5553

Blue River Bicycle Club
12311 State Line Road
Kansas City, MO 64145
816-942-4442

Capital City Cycling Club
PO Box 1202
Holts Summit, MO 65043
573-896-5222
www.capitolcitycyclingclub.com

Central Missouri Cycling Club
1516 Paris Road
Columbia, MO 65201
573-886-9258

Clayton Cycling Club
7811 Clayton Road
St. Louis, MO 63117
314-645-4447

Columbia Bicycle Club
PO Box 110
Columbia, MO 65205
573-446-3056
www.columbiabikeclub.com

Dirt Gypsies/Women's Riding
Network
1901 Ridge Lane
Pacific, MO 63069
636-707-4422

Folks on Spokes
734 Strafford Ridge Drive
Manchester, MO 63021
636-861-0558

Fulton Bicycle Club
www.fultonbicycle.com

Gateway Off-Road Cyclists
www.gorctrails.com

Johnson County Bicycle Club
www.jcbikeclub.org
Kansas City Bicycle Club
PO Box 412163
Kansas City, MO 64141
816-436-5606
www.kcbc.org

Kirksville Bicycle Club
218 W. Clark
La Plant, MO 63549

Lasers Cycling Club
1226 Havenhurst Road
Manchester, MO 63011

McDonnel D Bicycle Club
2901 Olde Gloucester Dr.
St. Charles, MO 63301

Missouri Fat Tire Series
5126 NE Antioch
Kansas City, MO 64119
816-455-2453

Ozark Cycling Club
2246 S. Kansas
Springfield, MO 65807
417-886-0080
www.ozarkcyclingclub.org

Ozark Off Road Cyclists
www.ozarkoffroadsyslists.com

Ozark Mtn Soul Riders
PO Box 1686
Lake Ozark, MO 65049
573-348-6221

Parkland Cycling Club
202 7th Street
Farmington, MO 63640
www.parklandcyclists.com

Plat Tire Hillbillies
3926 Hwy 54, Ste 100
Osage Beach, MO 65065
573-348-6221

Polk County Cycle Club
www.polkcountybikeclub.org

River City Pedallers
12011 Manchester Road
Des Peres, MO 63131
314-965-1447

Rolla Bicycle Association
40 Hawthorne Road
Rolla, MO 65401

Spokes and Spandex Bike Club
www.spokesandspandex.com

Springbike Bicycle Club
1134 S Cedarbrook Ave.
Springfield, MO 65804
417-882-9568
www.springbike.org

Springfield Cycling Club
3413 S. Hall Ave.
Springfield, MO 65804
417-882-3185
www.spfldcycling.org

St. Joseph Bicycle Club
2811 Duncan
St. Joseph, MO 64507
816-390-9703
www.stjoebikeclub.org

St. Louis BicycleWorks
4100 Shenandoah
St. Louis, MO
stlbwork@fastrans.net

St. Louis Cycling Club
12132 Wesmeade Dr.
Maryland Heights, MO 63043
314-739-5180
www.stlcc.net

St. Louis Mountain Bike Club
http://stlmtb.com

TC Tours
11816 St. Charles Rock Road
Bridgeton, MO 63044
314-739-5180
http://touringcyclist.com/tctours./
index.html

UMR Bike Club
202 University
Rolla, MO 65401
573-341-4209

Surfaced Trails

Mountain Bike Trails

Population Codes
❶=under 1,000 ❷=1,000-4,999 ❸=5,000-9,999
❹=10,000-49,999 ❺=50,000 and over

County to Trail Index

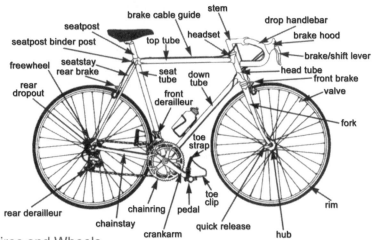

Tires and Wheels

Inspect your tire's thread for embedded objects, such a glass, and remove to avoid potential punctures.

Carry with you a spare tube, a patch kit, tire levers for removing the tire, and some duct tape.

Don't reassemble the wheel when fixing a flat until you have felt around the inside the tire. The cause of the puncture could still be lodged there.

Adjust your tire inflation pressure based on the type of ride. Lower pressure is better for off road biking or riding in the rain. A higher tire pressure is best for normal road biking or racing.

Sometimes a clicking sound is caused by two spokes rubbing together. Try a little oil on the spokes where they cross.

Reflectors

Have at least a rear reflector on your bike. Reflectors on the back of your pedals is an effective way of alerting motorists' to your presence.

Pedals

A few drops of oil to the cleat where it contacts the pedal will help silence those clicks and creaks in clipless pedals.

Saddles

Replace an uncomfortable saddle with one that contains gel or extra-dense foam. Select a saddle best designed for your anatomy. Women generally have a wider distance than men between their bones that contact the saddle top.

Chains and Derailleurs

Avoid combining the largest rear cog with the large chainring or the smallest cog with the small chainring.

Noises from the crank area may mean the chain is rubbing the front derailleur. To quiet this noise, move the front derailleur lever enough to center the chain through the cage but not cause a shift.

Find me a place, safe and serene,

Away from the terror I see on the screen.

A place where my soul can find some peace,

Away from the stress and the pressures released.

A corridor of green not far from my home

For fresh air and exercise, quiet will roam.

Summer has smells that tickle my nose

And fall has the leaves that crunch under my toes.

Beware, comes a person we pass in a while

with a wave and hello and a wide friendly smile.

Recreation trails are the place to be,

To find that safe haven of peace and serenity.

By Beverly Moore
Illinois Trails Conservancy

American Bike Trails publishes and distributes
maps, books and guides for the bicyclist.

For more information:
www.abtrails.com